Who's Looking at the Family?

Cover illustration:
from *The Found Image*
Institute of Contemporary
Family Photography
Alexander Honory
1989

Thomas Struth
*The Ghez Family,
Chicago*
1990
Courtesy
Galerie Max Hetzler
Berlin

Who's Looking

at the Family?

Val Williams

An exhibition selected by
Val Williams, Carol Brown
and Brigitte Lardinois

Barbican Art Gallery
1994

All the conventions

To make this fort a:

The furniture of ho

Lest we should see

Lost in a haunted w

Children afraid of t

Who have never be

W.H. Auden
From 'September 1, 1939'

onspire

ime

e ;

nere we are,

od,

night

happy or good.

Gerry Anderson presents
Candy and Andy 1967 - 68
photographed by Doug Luke
Collection Alan Dein

This publication
is dedicated to the memory of
Nathalie Crompton-Roberts
by her colleagues and friends at
Barbican Art Gallery

Contents

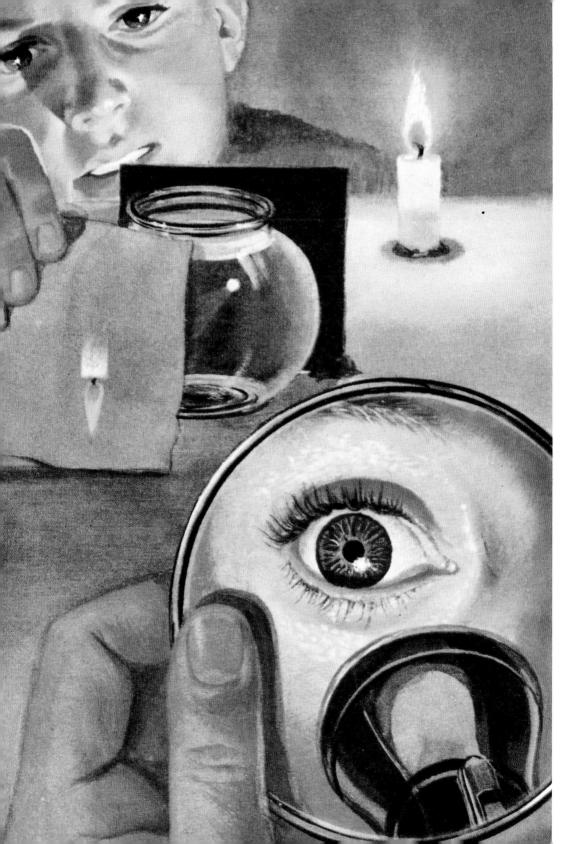

Artists

Jananne Al-Ani
Gerry Anderson and Doug Luke
Tina Barney
Richard Billingham
Anna and Bernhard Blume
Terry, Nick, Astrid, Austin
    and Maxwell Boorman
Florence Chevallier
Daguerreotypists of the 19th Century
Linda Duvall
Bruce Gilden
Jim Goldberg
Robert F. Hammerstiel
Anthony Haughey
John Heatley, Lancashire Constabulary
Alexander Honory
Lafayette, London and Manchester Studios
Ouka Lele
Susan Lipper
Katrina Lithgow
The Apes of London Zoo
Mari Mahr
Sally Mann
Corinne Noordenbos
Tony O'Shea
Martin Parr
Paul Reas
Liz Rideal
Thomas Ruff
Joachim Schmid
Margriet Smulders
John Stezaker
Thomas Struth
Larry Sultan
John R.J. Taylor
Nick Waplington
Carrie Mae Weems
Harry Wingfield
Aki Yamamoto

Harry Wingfield
illustration
from *Light, Mirrors
and Lenses*
Ladybird Junior Science Book
1962

Thomas Gainsborough
The Baillie Family
c.1784
Tate Gallery, London

Who *is* Looking at the Family?

For the most part we can only report what people say they do,
which is not the same as they actually do.
Michael Young and Peter Willmott:
Family and Kinship in East London
[Penguin Books, Harmondsworth]
1957

In 1784, Thomas Gainsborough painted a portrait of the Baillie
family. The work consisted of a tableau of three children, a baby in
arms, a father and a mother. Seated in the centre of the composition
a mother holds her baby for perusal by the artist, behind her the father
leans casually against a chair, part of the group, yet irrevocably distant
from it. It is a family portrait with a multitude of meanings –
expressions of unity and difference, of wealth and elevated social
standing as much as a picture of intimately related individuals.
We all retain images of family portraiture in our minds – no longer,
perhaps, the *pièce de résistance* in oils, but fragments, often
photographic, of times, days, people and incidents, retained only
through the persistence of memory.

Flicking through our memories for images of the family, we alight
on common visions: a birthday, a wedding, a holiday long gone.
Or perhaps some fading awareness of a holy scene, the Virgin Mary
beatific with her child, the solemn clustering of shepherds around a
makeshift cradle, or an unexpected gathering of kings. We may find
paintings, glimpsed in the hushed surroundings of an art gallery, their

pomp and certainties framed by the gravitas of gilt. In a leather-bound photograph album, bought out of curiosity on a market stall, we might come across a family group, gathered together for the sake of portraiture, an anonymous set of people, stranded in their histories by the passing of time.

Images are conjured up like genies; rub the lamp of memory and they are there, to grant our wishes. Confronted by these wilful spirits, we ask perhaps for elegy, or for revision, for reminders of the past, or even for forgetfulness.

From the beginning of photography, the family has been a focus of attention. From the mirrored surface of a daguerreotype, Victorian families gaze out at us, conscious perhaps of their confrontation with this new and marvellous tool of the camera. Their sense of posterity is acute. Through the milky tones of 19th-century albumen prints, we can decipher family groups gathered outside majestic homes, demonstrating their wealth and circumstance. As understanding of photographic technology increased, photography gradually became available to a wider number, and the snapshot elbowed its populist way onto the cultural and social agenda, making representation available, if still not to everybody, to a rapidly growing group of people.

Snapshot photography, seemingly so open and so casual, operates by its own clearly delineated rules, and families across the Western world used it to create a favourable reflection of domestic life. The stern gaze of the Victorians was replaced by an infallible smile. Snapshots mirrored family life as it ought to be, or as what we would wish it to be. Carefully coded, they acted as a talisman against the real.

As economic depression extended across the West in the Thirties, the family became a perfect channel for the expression of social angst. In the USA, documentarists such as Dorothea Lange and Walker Evans travelled across the American dustbowl to photograph a population under stress. Lange's seminal photograph *Migrant Mother* of 1936 (taken while she was working for the Farm Security Administration project) was a reworking of the ancient symbol of mother and child and stands to this day as the most iconic of modern madonnas (overleaf).

The traumas of the Second World War, of the Holocaust and the fragmentation and partition of Europe, were counteracted, or disguised, by post-war photographers with the adoption of a new internationalism. In 1951, the *Family of Man* exhibition opened at New York's Museum of Modern Art. A massive display of humanistic photojournalism, it attempted, with much panache, to paper over the cracks of a deeply damaged society. But hardly had the exhibition

Dorothea Lange
Migrant Mother
1936
Library of Congress
Washington DC

completed its international tour, than a new generation of
photographers, most markedly in the United States, began to peer
with a probing curiosity not into a generalized concept of family, but
into real lives. In 1965, New York photographer Diane Arbus
photographed parents and children for *Esquire* magazine ('Familial
Colloquies', July 1965). Arbus's portraits were stark and severe; the
actress Jayne Mansfield embraced her daughter Jayne Marie as if for
the first time; the writer, Susan Sontag and her son posed as two
unsmiling models of precocity. Three years later, in November 1968,
the London *Sunday Times* published Arbus's story 'Two American
Families' and the photographs were studies in dislocation. 'The
family' wrote Arbus of one of her subjects 'is undeniably close in a
painful, heartrending sort of way'. Of families in general, she wrote
'I think all families are creepy in a way'.[1]

    Her photographs marked the opening of a Pandora's box of
imagery. In Britain, in the Seventies, photographers continued to
probe into the nation's ills, often working in areas of intense
deprivation. But often this anxiety was combined with an acute
nostalgia for the passing of tradition. The family became an important
issue for the emerging discipline of sociology and for the mass media.

    By the beginning of the Eighties, nostalgia no longer seemed
appropriate. A heady period of prosperity, followed by economic
decline, engendered a pervasive state of confusion. The family, so
long seen as a national bedrock, faced new challenges. Issues
surrounding child abuse, domestic violence, the growing divorce rate

1.
Letters to
Peter Crookston,
then an editor
at the *Sunday Times*
1968

and single parenthood, together with dissention about lesbian mothers, test tube babies, surrogate motherhood, third world adoptions and arranged marriages, all became matters for public and private debate.

Photography is a responsive medium and photographers, reflecting the confusions of our times, began to portray the family in a multitude of ways. For some, interest lay in their own families, and in the complex social engineering which determines their structure. They used photography to probe familial relationships which were bewildering and full of mystery. Some employed the medium as an act of homage, as a comic device, or even as a tool for revenge. In family photography, there were no more rules. Old snapshots were brought out and re-viewed, in the hope that they would provide clues to the past. Lost childhoods were remembered, the fears and delights of parenthood minutely examined. Closed doors were opened and memories exhumed. Opening locked diaries of secrets, photographers sometimes turned a page and invited the world to take a look.

This exhibition takes as its core family photography made from the mid-Eighties to the present day. In the construction of this project, we have not attempted anthropology, nor have we aimed to present a snapshot of the family, or to comment on the state of the nation. We neither argue for the family nor against it, but merely acknowledge that it is there. *Who's Looking at the Family?* asks some questions, but does not presume to supply the answers. This collection of photographs is concerned with the present, but also makes links with the past; photographic history, despite its relative brevity, is cyclical and made up of constantly recurring motifs and configurations. In a postmodern culture, the past loses its precise chronological identity, and art becomes not so much a procession of traditions, but a system of signs adapted and adopted to fit a cultural mood.

Martin Parr
Love Cubes 1972
(see p. 115 for key

The Symmetry of Pairs

It is ignorance, our ignorance of one another, that creates this
terrifying erotic chaos. Information, a crumb of information,
seems to light the world.

The Journals of John Cheever
[Knopf, New York]
1990

In 1972, Martin Parr, then a photography student at Manchester
Polytechnic, decided to photograph couples he met on the street.
He portrayed them standing together, and then photographed them
on their own (pp. 16-17). From these pictures, he made *Love Cubes*,
a board game in which we are asked to place the individuals in their
correct pairs. Playing *Love Cubes*, we are obliged to consider our
notions of who should rightfully go with whom. The process is a
perplexing one – does an attractive woman fit with a handsome man
or do people with glasses necessarily gravitate to each other? *Love
Cubes* brings prejudices and preconceptions to the fore. When we try
to piece together this perplexing puzzle, do we maintain a strict
heterosexuality in our couple-making, or do we place woman with
woman, or male with male? *Love Cubes* is a conundrum; it is as much
to do with Us as it is with Them. Couples are families in embryo,
fragile partnerships founded on liking and on need, a staging point
between the self and the group; Parr's series, and the guesses which
he asks us to make about it can only emphasize that fragility.

Separated from *Love Cubes* by several decades, are the couples
photographed by the Lafayette studios in London and Manchester
during the Twenties and Thirties. These young people are less casual
than those Parr met in the 1970s; prepared for their weddings, they
face the camera with a more complex knowledge of their situation.
The men wear dark suits, the women wear white and, suitably
costumed, they become part of a drama for which they know the script
but have not yet deciphered the plot.

German photographic historian and curator Joachim Schmid has
been collecting family photographs for some time now. His
photographs of couples, assembled in complicated tableaux taken
from an archive 'dedicated to the trivial'[2] include pairings different
again from those photographed by Parr and the Lafayette studios
(pp. 20-21). Observing German families of the Fifties, many of whom
were children during the Second World War, issues of collective
memory become pervasive. Timm Starl, writing of the history of the
snapshot in Germany, charts the renaissance of the genre after 1945.

2.
Joachim Schmid,
'The World of Pictures':
introduction to *Taking
Snapshots : Amateur
Photography in Germany
from 1900 to the Present,*
German Institute for
Foreign Cultural
Relations
1993

Nothing, he said,

> *seemed worth preserving in a photograph : imprisonment, the*
> Trümmerfrauen *(women who worked clearing the rubble), the*
> *repatriated returning in endless lines, trading on the black market,*
> *all this demanded a kind of participation not really possible via the*
> *camera. Later, when life began to return to normal, there were again*
> *motifs found worth photographing : the new furniture and fittings, the*
> *new car, moving into a new house, the first television set. These, the*
> *fruits of industriousness, were what mattered now and so they were*
> *recorded and the prints stuck into albums often right next to the*
> *photographs taken on the last home leave.*[3]

3.
Ibid :
catalogue essay

The couples that Schmid has found, in his eclectic reassembling of
'naive' imagery, are lost in an uncertain idyll. Their ordinariness is
extraordinary as they pose against trees, or on a lakeside, or in the
sparkling interior of a brand new home. History stops, or is
momentarily forgotten, and unexpected sunlight beams out from a
world of shadows. Anonymous family photography of this kind,
divorced from its private context, becomes part of a universalised
fiction and a national narrative.

The private lives of couples are usually hidden from our gaze.
In Florence Chevallier's series *Le Bonheur*, we take notice of the
narcissism which operates within close pairs. Chevallier's
photographs are self-portraits of herself and her partner, and become
an elegantly wrought performance, directed to us, as audience (pp. 22,
23). Perhaps they form a logical codicil to the work of Parr, the
Lafayette studios and the family portraits from Fifties Germany. If
those earlier couples display an endearing gaucherie (at which we may
laugh and reassure ourselves of our sophistication), Chevallier's
knowing duo incite a certain anxiety as we enter into their ideal world
of luxury and abundance. Chevallier layers colour upon colour, tone
upon tone, surface upon surface, as we accompany this glamorous pair
through a world of good taste and stunning locations.

But there is a sharp edge beneath the surface glamour, there is
distance and malaise, narcissism and confusion. A man studies a
woman lying in the grass and we are unsure whether he is a guard
or a satyr; giant poppies lie across her breast – a stain of blood or a
tribute to beauty? Alone in their bedroom, these two people are
conscious of the difficult agendas implicit in relationships, and ponder
the consequences of their union. They appear to know what
photography means, realise its implications and the endless
permutations of motive. Family photography turned in upon itself,
mutated by a myriad of interpretations.

Previous page:
Joachim Schmid
from the series *Archive*
1986-94

Florence Chevallier
from the series *Le Bonheur*
1991-92

Florence Chevallier
from the series *Le Bonheur*
1991-92

23

Lost and Found in the Family:
Tales of Effects

So the Emperor walked in the procession under the beautiful
canopy, and everybody in the streets and at the windows said:
'Lord! How splendid the Emperor's new clothes are. What a
lovely train he has to his coat! What a beautiful fit it is!'
Nobody wanted to be detected seeing nothing: that would
mean he was no good at his job, or that he was very stupid.
None of the Emperor's costumes had ever been such a success.
'But he hasn't got anything on!', said a little child. 'Lor! just
hark at the innocent', said its father. And one whispered to the
other what the child had said: 'That little child there says he
hasn't got anything on'.
'Why, he hasn't got anything on!' the whole crowd was
shouting at last; and the Emperor's flesh crept, for it seemed
to him they were right. 'But all the same' he thought to
himself, 'I must go through with the procession'. So he held
himself more proudly than before, and the lords in waiting
walked on bearing the train – the train that wasn't there at all.

From *The Emperor's New Clothes*
in *Hans Christian Andersen : Forty-Two Stories*
Translated by M.R. James
[Faber and Faber Ltd, London, 1968]

In markets and second-hand shops throughout Europe, the effects of
the dead or the dispersed are laid out for public inspection. Among
those who browse are people with an interest in photography. From
the hundreds of images which lie in boxes and albums, some seem
especially attractive. From the clutter, faces stare out which demand
rescue.

Images without provenance inhabit an eerie territory within the
art world. In his search for photographs, Joachim Schmid has
collected snapshots which, by their structure and content, bear
remarkable resemblance to the work of 'great' photographers. He has
found an Ansel Adams here and a Paul Strand there, and makes a
comedy out of the random nature of curatorship.

Found photography disclaims authorship, and by selection and
presentation, new 'authors' are found. Historians and archivists invest
these ownerless images with their own fictions, and allow us, as
audience, to develop our own.

The Lost Child is such a case in point (opposite). Found on a
market stall in the East End of London in 1993, its history is
unknown. It is a fading snapshot of a poorly dressed child with wide,
inquisitive eyes; enclosed in an elaborate frame, it emerges as an
enigma. Because of its ambivalence, we can invest it with our own

Photographer unknown
Untitled [The Lost Child]
Collection Val Williams

drama. The photograph has travelled from a private sphere to a public one; deprived of its original context, it has become an art object of an idiosyncratic kind.

Found photography is an effective antidote to the notion of reputation. Taken up by artists such as Christian Boltanski and John Stezaker, it becomes part of some universalist art work. Boltanski has used found photography to examine the resonances of the Holocaust, while Stezaker, in his *Spanish Collages* (1985-87) (pp. 28, 29) explores the high kitsch of Catholicism to present the Holy Family in a way which is half sardonic, half reverential. In his 1990 series *Care*, Stezaker has employed found photography in the telling of particular narratives. Art historian David Mellor has written:

Care *stages a phantasy about home and the nurturing of children that lures the spectator inside the frightening scenario of a Grimm's tale . . . An estranged boy and girl are complemented by two larger, parental figures. The uncanny element lies in the fact that these parents are absences, cutouts, silhouettes – not black and blank, in this case, but composed of forestry, a northern wood. This woodland glade is almost idyllic with shafting sunbeams . . . almost, for this is nevertheless the terrain of magicians, the no-man's land of 'The Wood Between the Worlds' that occurs in C. S. Lewis's* The Magician's Nephew.

As a child in the West Midlands town of Worcester in the early 1950s, Stezaker grew up in the shadows of an advertisement hoarding for 'Start Rite' shoes: in his words 'it haunted my childhood'. As paradigms of the welfarist construction of the British child, the poster children were seen from behind, walking off down the endless road of life, 'from the cradle to the grave', in the phrase used by the post-war Labour party to typify the all-encompassing care that the Welfare State would lavish on its subjects. Such an infinity of care, like the woodland glade in Care *was, to Stezaker, positively sinister.*[4]

Mellor cites Stezaker's photomontages as giving 'access to his childhood phantasies of absence, loss and fear'.[5] Even more phantasmagorical is the domestic scenario of *Candy and Andy* (pp. 7, 34, 35), created (for a series of comic books) by Gerry Anderson and Doug Luke in the Sixties, and rediscovered by oral historian and collector Alan Dein in 1993. Candy and Andy are a pair of life-sized dolls who live in an English village with Mr and Mrs Bearanda, two giant pandas. Alan Dein has written of this remarkable 'family':

Their relationship is unstated. We are not told whether the Panda bears are their parents, foster parents, or guardians. The 'family' own a magic toy shop in Riverdale, a fantasy English village whose

4.
Film Still Collages, exhibition catalogue F. GG, Frankfurt 1990

5.
Ibid.

*inhabitants are craftsmen, shopkeepers, fishermen and lots of children
. . . As in most successful children's stories, the adult characters are
almost subordinate, less in control. Most of the adventures in* Candy
and Andy *are mundane domestic accidents . . . and it is the adults
who get into the tangles.*[6]

6.
Unpublished synopsis
of the history of
Candy and Andy
by Alan Dein
1994

The scenarios of *Candy and Andy* describe a world in which children
transgress the boundaries of 'normal' behaviour. They take fireworks
from strangers and exchange dark and glazed looks across their bear-
parents' heads. In their absence and disdain, they are like aliens from
another planet, with no regard for the rules of adulthood. When
accidents happen, Candy and Andy take charge, and when the
Bearandas go to sleep, their doll children stay awake and alert. In their
intelligence and their secrecy, they are the children of nightmares.

Alien to conventional notions of childhood too are Linda Duvall's
photographs of *Babies That Look Alike* (1991 and 1994) (pp. 32-33).
Duvall has combed a local paper in Canada, *The Windsor Star*, to find
birth notices of new-born infants whose faces appear exactly alike.
She has observed how new parents have promoted these unformed
beings to the status of adults by predicting their future careers. She
has also noted the detailed naming of family members within the text
of these notices, an affirmation of the process of lineage. Duvall's
Babies That Look Alike confound our notions of the individuality of
the infant persona. Frighteningly identical, they invade our
consciousness like creatures from outer space.

In 1989, German curator Alexander Honory made a compilation
of christening photographs bought at a flea market in Cologne
(pp. 36-37). Commenting on Honory's exploration of family
photography, Rolf Sachsse makes the following observations:

*Alexander Honory is an artist who was born in Germany and trained
in Poland. He is a Polish filmaker on German television. Such
paradoxes can be taken further in his curriculum vitae, but that does
not concern us here. For German spectators, it is quite obvious that
the photographs stem from Poland. For Polish spectators, the
protagonists in the photographs could equally be indubitably
German. The artist keeps his sources to himself and everyone is left
with his own assumptions, including myself. Dress and body language
are media of social envy but are certainly no guarantee of one's place
on the national ladder if this is still relevant nowadays. How
frighteningly topical such considerations can be is apparent in the
actions taken by German extremists on buildings in Germany that
are inhabited by foreign citizens.*[7]

7.
From catalogue
Das Gefundene Bild,
Ministry of the Flemish
Community,
KMSK/ICC –
International Cultureel
Centrum, Antwerp
1994

Found photography, it would seem, belongs to everybody, and to
nobody at all.

Discovered in an entirely different way were the family album photographs of Mrs Hilda Thompson and her daughters June and Hilda (opposite). In the spring of 1988, June and Hilda Thompson shot and killed their father Tommy, a man who had violently abused them throughout their lives. During the course of her research into the lives of the Thompsons,[8] author Alexandra Artley became fascinated by the family's photograph albums:

8.
For her book
Murder in the Heart,
Hamish Hamilton, London
1993

It was the family photographs, particularly those taken during June and Hilda Thompson's primary-school days, that became some of the most painful things to examine in the history of this family. For many months after first meeting the Thompson women, I had actually avoided the place in my room in Glasgow where, after returning as usual one night from Preston, I had set down in a carrier bag the cache of family snaps meticulously labelled, filed in white envelopes and then double-wrapped in clear plastic by June Thompson herself with her strange silent efficiency. For a long time, I did not want to go near those photographs and the reason was this – the children in them not only looked perfectly normal, they could have been me or my friends at that age . . .

That afternoon in Glasgow, as I turned on through the first packet of Thompson family snaps, I next came across an almost identical school photograph of June's younger sister, Hilda – the perhaps more hesitantly smiling portrait of a child whose father had already held her right hand close to the flames of an open coal fire until the scorch of her screams had taught her never again to go near the fireside and, indeed, still prevents her from daring to light the gas ring of an ordinary kitchen stove. But with artless people's compulsive willingness to smile in everyday snapshots, there was still no clue in this photograph to the domestic reality of the Thompson children's lives. To me, always dubious about visual appearances as a way of ever knowing the truth, these conventional family photographs confirmed that one may smile and smile and be a victim.[9]

9.
Ibid. pp. 139–140

Artley's bewilderment on first examining the Thompson family photographs emerges from our somewhat naive, but nevertheless deeply held, belief in the veracity of snapshots. Tommy Thompson's photographs of his severely damaged children acted as propaganda, both within and outside the family, and positioned him as a seemingly loving storyteller who dealt, persuasively, in idylls.

From an abandoned portrait on a market stall to the holiness of a Spanish postcard re-arranged and re-contextualised, ending with an innocuous family album which slowly yields up its secrets of dysfunction, found photography provides both evidence and disinformation; confusing and enlightening, it has many meanings . . .

THE TOWER
Blackpool

June and Hilda Thompson, Blackpool,
aged six and four respectively
July 1958

June and Hilda Thompson with Beauty
1 July 1958

June and Hilda Thompson
with their pet rabbit
June 1958

June Thompson
May 1959

BEACH (nee Clelland)–Scott and Barb are happy to announce the arrival of their first child, a beautiful baby girl, Megan Suzanne, born on Friday Sept. 13, 1991 at 12:32 p.m., weighing 8 lbs. 14½ oz. Proud grandparents, Jim & Mildred Clelland and 1st time grandparents, Larry & Marg Beach. Special thanks to Dr. J. Jones and the Med Student, as well as Gail and the rest of the 3rd Floor Staff at Grace.

POISSON/SAUTER--Bob and Ingrid thank God for the safe arrival of their son, Bradley Robert, on Oct. 18, 1991, weiging 8 lbs. 5 oz., 2:42 p.m. Proud 1st time grandparents, Harry & Wilma Sauter and 11th time, Ed & Margaret Poisson. Also a special thanks to Alice & Dr. Wm. McLeod.

DUNNING-Mino–Shane and Tammy welcome with love their first baby a girl, Amanda Corinne Lorraine, weighing a healty, 7 lbs. 13 ozs. Aug. 21, 1991 at 10:33 p.m. 9th grandchild for Bernie and Bertha Dunning, 1st grandchild for Barry and Sandy Mino, 1st great grandchild for Russ and Rita Mino. 2nd great grandchild for Len and Joyce Letourneau. Daddy's doing fine. Special thanks to Dr. Glowacky and nursing staff at Met Maternity.

KRESAN-(GAUGHA Daddy's little boy is fi here. Frank Joseph was on August 8th, 1991 weig 8lbs. 14oz. Proud parent Bill and Maureen. Proud time grandparents Frank Janice Kresan and 20th g child for Eugene and Ev line Gaughan. Proud g grandparents are Leonard Mae Austin. Thanks to doctors and nurses at M (Insured)

BERTS –Dr. Edwin &
ie (nee Topolie) welcome
love their son, COLE
EPH, 8 lb. 6 oz., on Aug.,
1991 at Metropolitan
pital. Precious baby broth–
r Kailey and Eddie. Proud
dparents Mr. & Mrs.
in Roberts, London and
& Mrs. John Topolie,
rmory.

MEYER –Brian and Frances
Lena (Fabiano) are happy to
announce the arrival of Carly
Katrina, born Thursday,
October 17, 1991 at Victoria
Hospital, London at 12:35
p.m., 7 lbs., 6½ ozs. Proud
grandparents Peppino and
Caterina Fabiano, Donna
Stewart, Calvin and Vera
Meyer. Ryan and Caitlin are
thrilled, Cinda sends an XO.
All the children would like to
wish Mommy and Daddy a
Happy 10th Anniversary,
October 24, 1991 and also a
Happy 71st Birthday to Non-
no, October 21, 1991. Special
thanks to Aunt Laurie.

MORGAN –Jim and Carol
(nee Shuel) would like to announce the birth of their
daughter, Caitlyn Joyce, 6 lbs.
6 ozs. at Met Hospital, on June
27, 1991. First-time grandparents are Marie & Walter Shuel
and Nancy & Jeff Derkatz.
Special thanks to Joelyn, and
Dr. McLeod.

QUINT –John and Audrey are
happy to announce the safe
arrival of their son, Jonathan
Andrew, on July 9, 1991. Play-
mate for Elise. Great-grand-
mothers Mrs. Theresa Mayer
and Mrs. Katharina Quint.
Grandparents Mr. and Mrs.
Leon Cyr and Mr. and Mrs.
Anton Quint.

This page and opposite:
Gerry Anderson presents
Candy and Andy 1967-68
photographed by Doug Luke
Collection Alan Dein

Overleaf:
Institute of Contemporary Family Photography
Alexander Honory
The Found Image
1989

My Father, My Son

In the first place, the theory that my father was omniscient or infallible was now dead and buried. He probably knew very little; in this case he had not known a fact of such importance that if you did not know that, it could hardly matter what you knew. My Father, as a deity, as a natural force of immense prestige, fell in my eyes to a human level. In future, his statements about things in general need not be accepted implicitly.

Edmund Gosse: *Father and Son*
[Heinemann, London]
1907

In 1993, colour documentarist Paul Reas decided to embark on an unusual exercise in genealogy and began his *Portrait of an Invisible Man*, a series of photographs about his father which would, he hoped, begin to repair, or at least explain, the experiences of his lonely and damaged childhood (pp. 39, 40). Paul Reas has written:

For thirty-eight years I have carried this man inside me. He is a man I recognise but know nothing about. He is a man with no known history. A man of secrets and suspicion. A detached man. A lonely man? A man of greed and sarcasm. A silent man. A man of hypocrisy. A man of lies and double standards. An unemotional man. A dying man. The man is my father . . .

For as long as I can remember my father has been an 'absent presence' in my life. Only ever there on Sundays and even then a sleeping, silent figure in an armchair. Who was this man? Where did he go? 'The official line' – he was a door-to-door salesman travelling the country. 'The mystery' – why did he never take an overnight bag? 'The suspicion' – had he another life somewhere else?[10]

Making this series of photographs, Paul Reas has opened his own chamber of revelations. He has challenged sacred family institutions – the patriarchy, the silence and the keeping of secrets – in his attempt to uncover a hidden history. And he has done it by photographing the microcosm which a child observes in the macrocosm of home – a trapped moth in the silver shining cobwebs above a lavatory cistern emphasises the fragility of a child's freedoms, the detritus which hides itself beneath the clean surface of every family story. Reas pictures his mother (who supported the entire family from her earnings as a cleaner) by showing her hands wielding a dustpan and brush, for in this family, her role was labourer and breadwinner and her presence counteracted a patriarchal absence. For Paul Reas, childhood resulted in a grave injury, which perhaps these photographs may begin to repair:

10.
Unpublished papers
sent to the author
1993

38

Paul Reas
from *Portrait of an Invisible Man*
1993 - 94

Paul Reas
from *Portrait of an Invisible Man*
1993 - 94

11.
Ibid.

So now here I am, so many unanswered questions, so much confused
emotion, no sense of identity – and the man with all the answers living
out the last few years of his life. Like his diseased heart starved of
oxygen, I too am damaged.[11]

Paul Reas's meticulously constructed descriptions of domestic life
may perhaps exorcise demons, the ghouls and goblins which inhabit
a child's imagination; they are photography as remedy, as exhumation
and a personal adventure on a grand scale.

Though Larry Sultan's memories of family life have none of the
bleakness of *Portrait of an Invisible Man*, they are made with the same
spirit of inquiry (pp. 42-43). Sultan embarked upon this
autobiographical series in 1982 and has written of its genesis:

I was in Los Angeles visiting my parents. One night, instead of
renting a videotape, we pulled out a box of home movies that none
of us had seen in years. Sitting in the living room, we watched thirty
years of folktales – epic celebrations of the family. They were
remarkable, more like a record of hopes and fantasies than of actual
events. It was as if my parents had projected their dreams onto film
emulsion. I was in my mid-thirties and longing for the intimacy,
security, and comfort that I associated with home. But whose home?
Which version of the family?
When I began to photograph, I thought of this work as a portrait
of my father. In many ways, I still do. I can remember the peculiar
feeling I had looking at the first pictures that I made of him. I was
recreating him and, like a parent with an infant, I had the power
to observe him knowing that I would not be observed myself.
Photographing my father became a way of confronting my confusion
about what it is to be a man in this culture . . .
What drives me to continue this work is difficult to name. It has more
to do with love than with sociology, with being a subject in the drama
rather than a witness. And in the odd and jumbled process of working
everything shifts; the boundaries blur, my distance slips, the
arrogance and illusion of immunity falters. I wake up in the middle
of the night, stunned and anguished. These are my parents. From
that simple fact, everything follows. I realize that beyond the rolls

12.
Larry Sultan,
Pictures from Home,
Abrams, New York
1992

of film and the few good pictures, the demands of my project and my
confusion about its meaning, is the wish to take photography literally.
To stop time. I want my parents to live forever.[12]

The home movies which Larry Sultan watched with his parents on
that evening in 1982 now form an integral part of his photo-series
(p. 44). Printed as stills, they are a kaleidoscope of history, investing
the past with both magic and pathos. Appealing to the power of
photography to halt the passing of time, Sultan sees the process as

Larry Sultan
*My Mother
Posing for Me*
from the series
Pictures from Home
1984
Courtesy Janet Borden Inc.
New York

alchemic. When Sultan photographs his father, he contrasts the powerful, ebullient businessman of the Fifties and Sixties with the calm and somnolent man now in retirement. The photographs are allusive rather than literal and overwhelm the power of documentary. Larry Sultan has produced a portrait of a set of deeply intertwined and complicated relationships. When he looks at his father and mother he notes how balances have altered and symmetry has changed. The series is a catharsis, but of a very gentle kind.

Richard Billingham's photography marks the beginning rather than the end of a personal and aesthetic journey. His background, in the industrial West Midlands, was unsettled, and he has documented the domestic chaos which he encountered while living with his alcoholic father. Billingham's portraits of his father show malaise and tension but, though critical, they do not entirely condemn. In *Triptych of Ray*, made in 1991 (pp. 45, 46, 47), there are echoes of a more antique photography than one would expect to find in the 1990s, of Edward Curtis perhaps, or even Nadar. They are wistful portraits which have a certain nobility, captured on the edge of the abyss. There is little comfort to be found in Billingham's extensive and continuing documentation of family life, but there is acknowledgement and a kind of acceptance.

These three photo-series, mark a new departure in the way men photograph each other. They are profoundly moving documents of relationships between adults and between parents and their children, which reveal secrets, exposing raw nerves and hidden emotions.

Larry Sultan
Movie stills from the series *Pictures from Home*
Courtesy Janet Borden Inc.
New York

Richard Billingham
Triptych of Ray
1991
(see also overleaf)

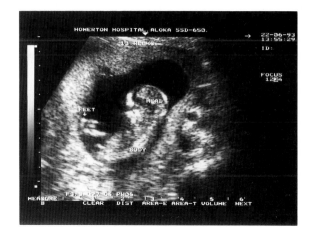

Calum as a Foetus
1993
Scan made after
13 weeks of pregnancy

Courtesy Barbara Conway
and David Brittain

Madonnae Ambiguae

She reminded me of a mountain covered with snow; at its summit the sun shone with warmth and splendour, and there was a sweetness and gaiety in the air. Further down the clouds gathered, plunging the lower, more arid slopes into darkness. At the centre of the mountain ran a deep river, glimpsed only at intervals, where it surged through a rift in the hillside with unexpected and disconcerting power.

Angelica Garnett writing about her mother, Vanessa Bell
in *Deceived with Kindness*,
[Chatto and Windus, The Hogarth Press, London]
1984

Motherhood is a state of ambivalence and a site of debate. Mothers and children have been painted and photographed since the beginning of both mediums, have been heroised for their virtue, pitied for their poverty, idealised for their beneficience. They have become symbols, in a patriarchy, of a still and nurturing presence. Artists and photographers have reflected all these images. Governments and propagandists have used them to reassure nations, to promote campaigns, to persuade and revise. When Suffragette photographer Nora Smyth photographed poor East End mothers before the First World War, she presented them as women who fought for survival. When socialist documentarist Edith Tudor-Hart visited these deprived areas of London in the Thirties, she used their poverty to campaign for improved conditions and better housing. In the Fifties, *Picture Post* photojournalist Grace Robertson was commissioned to photograph the birth of a baby. Her photographs (too graphic for women to see, her male editors believed) were never published in this 'family' magazine. More recently, a photograph by Annie Leibovitz, of the actress Demi Moore in an advanced state of pregnancy, appeared on the cover of *Vanity Fair* magazine (in 1993) and provoked a media debate about the acceptability of such an image. Society influences and to some extent controls the ways in which motherhood is represented.

Katrina Lithgow's photographs express great curiosity about the appearance of motherhood (pp. 50, 51). She portrays her subjects alone with their children – there are no couples in these scenarios, and if there *are* partners, they are off on some other adventure in a wider world. The women in Lithgow's portraits seem a little startled that she is there, an observer, with camera and concepts, of the close communion of mothers and their children. It is a quiet and still space which Lithgow photographs – we can perhaps faintly discern the ticking of a clock or the hum of afternoon traffic, but nothing more. And these women watch Lithgow as closely as she watches them, with a mutual question about motives and preoccupations. They are no coy madonnas, their arms show the strain of picking and carrying, their pregnant bodies are stretched and full as they wait for the moment of birth, and they bide their time with both impatience and humour. Katrina Lithgow's photographs are about looking and enquiring, they address questions of voyeurism and as quickly discard them.

Dutch photographer Margriet Smulders has chosen to look not at a still, calm world of domestica, but at a comedy, carried on between men, women and their children within the fantastical stage set of home (pp. 52, 53). Smulders' self portraits show her as a heroine who has subverted a carefully crafted plot, has looked at the script and decided that the lines need changing. Hers is a boisterous scenario, full of style and language, playing on pattern, surface and shape to construct a satire of domesticity. In one photograph, made when eight months pregnant, she poses as a languorous pin-up amongst a pile of scattered underwear, but her expression, querulous, embarrassed, belies the pose. In another self-portrait, Smulders lies on the shelf of a wardrobe, while her child plays beneath her. Both seem oblivious to each other, but the connection between the two is undoubted; lost in their own worlds of preoccupation and reflection, the identities of mother and child merge and then separate. Like all mothers of young children, Smulders seems to have a notion of both paradise and pain.

Ouka Lele's photographs are fantastical constructions (pp. 54, 55). Her Spanish interiors have none of the stillness of Lithgow's rooms or the comic possibilities of Smulders' photo-constructions. They are dark and romantic places, where babies lurk and one can come across rumours of angels. Ouka Lele paints on her photographs,

heightening colours and emphasising lines, encouraging the super real
and suggesting the surreal. The characters in her plots appear to have
no connection with each other, as they meander across a wild and
cluttered domestic landscape. Writing about her work, Ouka Lele
makes reference to Lewis Carroll and the dream which he invented
for his favourite child, Alice Liddell; like Alice, Ouka Lele is beguiled
by the potions which awake the imagination and take us beyond the
real.

These ambiguous madonnas and their offspring, photographed so
differently by three women, all from different cultures, remind us that
motherhood is a condition in which we invest emotions of many
different orders. It is a space for reflection and for riot, for peace and
labour, a central pillar of the family, yet always an enigma.

Katrina Lithgow
Esther and Rebecca
Twins, London
1992

Katrina Lithgow
*Sarah Pregnant with Lily
and Max, London*
1992

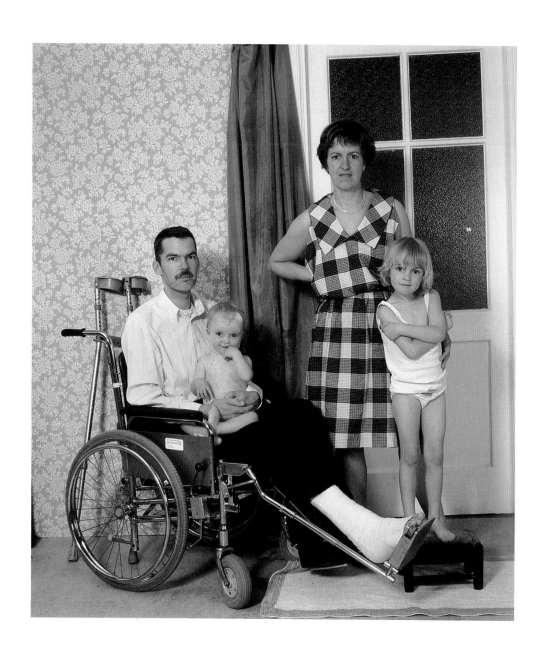

Margriet Smulders
Maternité X
1993

Margriet Smulders
Maternité IX
1992

Ouka Lele
Portrait of Ana Quadros
1986-87

Ouka Lele
Me levanto por la mañana
y hay un gran charco en mi casa
[I woke up in the morning
and found a large pool in my house]
1986

Watching Us Watching Them

The common bond between Us may be the Other. The Other
may not be even as localised as a definable Them that one can
point to . . . The Other is everyone's experience. Each person
can do nothing because of the Other. The Other is everywhere
elsewhere.

R.D. Laing
The Politics of Experience and the Bird of Paradise
[Penguin Books, Harmondsworth]
1967

When the Apes of London Zoo photographed the people who come
to stare through the bars of their cages, they had no idea of the process
of portraiture with which they were involved.[13] Of their subjects, we
can surmise a little more. The view from the cage is not a pleasant
one, for when people look at apes, they appear a little less than human.
Confronted by photographers, we try to make an impression, to look
our best perhaps, to show the finer side of our faces, to smile in an
engaging way. We are conscious that, through the lens of a camera,
we are encountering a member of our own species. When we regard
the apes, we cannot help but consider the Other.

13.
The Apes were provided
with cameras as part
of a *Telegraph Magazine*
picture story
1992

Photography is a medium of communication, and portraiture
even more so. A portraitist hopes, sometimes vainly, to find an essence
of a personality, conveyed through look and features. Subjects, in
their turn, subvert the process, presenting to their portrayers those
facts which they wish known and hiding more unpalatable truths. It
is a constantly circular process, in which both parties believe that they
may have the upper hand.

The photographs made by the Apes of London Zoo (opposite) are
much like the ones which we make for comedy in a photo booth.
Encouraged by the anonymity of the process, we grimace and gesture,
act to the camera in the secure knowledge that we are seen merely by
a machine. No-one knows what apes think when they see our human
family groups clustered outside their cages, observing their every
movement and their intimate lives, but the evidence produced by
these photographs presents us as an equal spectacle, and a greater
absurdity.

Photographs taken by
The Apes of London Zoo
1992
Telegraph Magazine
London

56

Empty Rooms, Deserted Spaces

The domestic interior has always held a particular fascination for
photographers. Homes are very personal places, littered with the
objects and artifacts which identify us both to ourselves and to the
world outside. They are conglomerations of both public and private
spaces – a collection of china in a cabinet is a spectacle worthy of
display to all, while the contents of a rubbish bin remain firmly
hidden. When photographers photograph home interiors, their
agendas are often quite clear. Working in the United States in the
Thirties, social documentarist Walker Evans documented the lives of
the rural poor, producing, as part of that narrative, a remarkable
collection of elegiac still lives, beguiling fragments presented as
roomscapes, monuments to poverty and to thrift. Later photographers
would use the home as a vehicle for social exploration. Martin Parr
and Daniel Meadows' 1973 photo-series *June Street* (made in Salford
and located near to the real 'Coronation Street'),[14] inspired by Bill
Owens' classic 1973 book *Suburbia*, was ostensibly a documentation
of family life in the north of England, but the rooms stole the show.
Parr and Meadows became fascinated by the rubber plants, coal fires
and electric wall clocks, three-piece-suites and carpets which formed
focal points in these tidy, well-ordered homes. Like explorers in a
foreign land, Parr and Meadows documented working-class life with
a spare and careful precision.

14.
Demolished just before
Parr and Meadows began
their photo-series

By the Eighties, home had become a focus for something more
obviously de-constructive. The loosening of traditional class and
family structures, a rise in property ownership and the growth of a
new meritocracy made the home a vehicle of aspirational dreams.
British photographers like Paul Reas, John Taylor, Ron O'Donnell,
Anna Fox and Martin Parr began to look at the home interior as a
system of signs – each pointing the way to ironic conclusions about
the structures which make up our everyday lives.

In the mid-Eighties, photographer John Taylor asked his sister
Brenda if he could photograph her home in suburban north London.
Taylor visited the house when all of the family, except for a large collie
dog, were out. The photographs which he made show an intense
curiosity, an inquisitiveness which verges gently on the transgressive

(pp. 60, 61). They are full of silence and surface as Taylor's gaze skims across shining glass and polished furniture, thick carpet and soft bedding. It is a picture not so much of privacy invaded, but of privacy explored. As we follow him through this quiet place, anxious to know its secrets, we are delighted for a moment by a glimpse of the contents of a bathroom cabinet, the ordered chaos of a family noticeboard, the odd shapes of worn shoes. Taylor has produced an anatomy of a family without our seeing the people who wear the shoes, who hoover the carpet, who maintain the gloss of the wood or the polish of the glass. Without their presence, we imagine their faces and their bodies, conjure up their voices and invest them with our own fictions. Curator Mark Haworth-Booth has written of the photographs included in *Ideal Home*:

> First of all, they make one put quotation marks around the word 'ordinary'. Without melodrama, the photographs insist on the importance of their subjects. Taken together, the photographs become absorbing. This is one of the few albums of photographs that one wishes would not come to an end. And, actually, the series continues in one's own imagination: instead of touring the domesticity of strangers one begins to ponder one's own habitat.[15]

15.
From introduction
to *Ideal Home*,
Cornerhouse, Manchester
1989

Though Taylor's family is portrayed here by their possessions and the domestic space which they have created, there is another insistent voice. When John Taylor completed *Ideal Home*, he asked his sister Brenda to comment on his representation. Her remarks, sometimes quizzical, sometimes providing information, sometimes disapproving, add a significant coda to this body of work. Photographers bring their own notions to whatever they photograph, selecting and disregarding as they see fit. The voice of the householder challenges the documentarist's power: 'You may have seen it like that', she seems to say, 'but I know how it really is'. Half documentary, half collaboration, *Ideal Home* emerges as a narrative of a particular time and a specific location, but its meanings are composite, its enigma intact.

Elsewhere in Europe, photographers looked as closely at the home interior for clues to their history. When German photographer Thomas Ruff wandered through the home of his family in Bavaria, he too searched for indications of lineage (pp. 64, 65). The Ruff house is calm and quiet, its smooth, pale walls revealing small icons of evidence, a religious artifact here, a family photograph there. It is a careful home, where everything has a designated and incontrovertible place, it has a confidence and an immense sense of propriety. Thomas Ruff is best known for his portraits, studies of faces which interrogate the photographer as much as he questions them, and in which a

59

John R.J. Taylor
Swing Bin Refuse
from *Ideal Home*
1985 - 89

Well, John takes some funny shots . . .
I'm kind of used to it . . .
That's Cheddar with chives . . . it was probably old and mouldy
and did not look appealing to me to cook with either.
I'm afraid that that apple belonged to my daughter . . .
I recognise . . . the baby teeth marks.
She was then five or six.
She didn't have a fierce appetite then . . .
That apple would never have happened today . . .
that would have been devoured along with
the cheese.

Brenda Nicola

John R.J. Taylor
Rear Bedroom under Redecoration (Adidas Training Shoes)
from *Ideal Home*
1985 - 89

The chair is from the dining room suite . . .
I told him basically what I wanted and it was delivered.
I looked at it and I realized it wasn't my cup of tea
but for the price I had to keep it . . .
because it was very reasonable.
I hate it when it's being decorated . . .
I hate being unorganized, but when I have the time
I enjoy decorating, myself, but I hate to see the mess . . .
I don't think that's an uncommon feeling,
amongst women anyway.

Brenda Nicola

careful distance is maintained. Photographing his family home, one can sense this same important space between photographer and subject, a curiosity tempered by respect.

Police photographer John Heatley had a very different agenda from that of Taylor and Ruff when he photographed the Thompson family home in Skeffington Road, Preston, in 1988 (opposite). When Heatley documented its contents, he too was collecting evidence, but of a much more tragic nature. After the killing of Tommy Thompson by his two daughters, June and Hilda, Heatley was called in to make a record of the scene. As he walked through the rooms, he photographed a man lying dead on the bed, as if asleep. He opened drawers and photographed their contents, discovered a store cupboard in which all the items were labelled, noted a hole in the plastic bathtub made by a shotgun. Like a cartographer mapping some alien and terrifying land, he identified the surface of dysfunction and exposed a terrible history. Found in the family, in a small terraced house, were disclosures of the loss of innocence and the theft of comfort.

These photographers have opened doors and revealed secrets, some of which are the meat of comedy and the products of affection, others which show a dense and unfathomable human tragedy. For a moment, perhaps for years, we hold these pictures in our memories; they tell us a little about other people, and a great deal about ourselves.

John Heatley
Interior of the Thompson family home
193 Skeffington Road, Preston
1988
Lancashire Constabulary

Thomas Ruff
Interior 1979

Thomas Ruff
Interior 1979

Thomas Ruff
Interior 1979

Thomas Ruff
Interior 1981

Thomas Ruff
Interior
1979

Nearly Narrative:
Some Domestic Stories

Home is so sad. It stays as it was left,
Shaped to the comfort of the last to go
As if you win them back. Instead, bereft
of anyone to please, it withers so,
Having no heart to put aside the theft

And turn again to what it started as,
A joyous shot at how things ought to be,
Long fallen wide. You can see how it was:
Look at the pictures and the cutlery.
The music in the piano stool. That vase.

Philip Larkin: 'Home is So Sad', 31 December 1958
From *The Whitsun Weddings : Poems by Philip Larkin.*
[Faber and Faber Limited, London]
1964

Our conception of home is perhaps more than anything, a system of memories. Half-remembered childhoods, the faces of once young parents, a treasured toy, long since lost, a photograph or a tattered child's book bring back memories of home and family which echo across the spaces of adulthood, bringing us sharply up against the past. Diaries form a narrative of the past, extrapolate from the facts and create a personal history. Photography narrates stories of the real world, and in doing so, makes that world both more and less real. When photograph and journal meet, stories are constructed which set imaginative agendas acting as touchstones for our own experience and our own fictions.

When New York photographer Susan Lipper set out to photograph the lives of the people of the small rural settlement of Grapevine, in the Appalachian mountains of West Virginia, she saw her photographs as 'not an effort to document, in any real sense . . . but rather the collision of my experiences, the tangible world and the nature of photography' (pp. 68, 69).[16] Looking back on her time in Grapevine, Lipper recalls that 'it was almost like a fairy tale, the way things are meant to be, and there they really were'.[17] Going beyond documentary, Lipper produces a photography which interprets rather then describes.

Sally Mann's series of photographs of her three children, Emmett, Jessie and Virginia were made not many miles away from Grapevine but tell a very different saga of American family life (pp. 71, 72). Mann writes of her work:

> *These are photographs of my children living their lives here too. Many of these pictures are intimate, some are fictions and some are fantastic, but most are of ordinary things every mother has seen – a wet bed, a bloody nose, candy cigarettes. They dress up, they pout and posture, they paint their bodies, they dive like otters in the dark river.*

16.
From *Grapevine : Photographs by Susan Lipper*, Cornerhouse, Manchester 1994

17.
In conversation with the author January 1994

Thomas Ruff
House no.9, I
1989

66

Susan Lipper
from the *Grapevine* series
1991

Susan Lipper
from the *Grapevine* series
1991

They have been involved in the creative process since infancy. At times, it is difficult to say exactly who makes the pictures. Some are gifts to me from my children : gifts that come in a moment as fleeting as the touch of an angel's wing . . .

When the good pictures come, we hope they tell truths, but truths 'told slant' just as Emily Dickinson commanded. We are spinning a story of what it is to grow up. It is a complicated story and sometimes we try to take on the grand themes : anger, love, death, sensuality and beauty. But we tell it all without fear and without shame.[18]

18.
From text by Sally Mann in her book *Immediate Family*, Phaidon, London 1992

Sally Mann's family story is a dark narrative of romance and mystery. There are dragons and monsters which stalk the calm Virginian woods, and Sally Mann, fearful of some primitive magic, takes their presence seriously. Hers are women's stories, fables of some other time, told in the sunlight, but ever mindful of doubt and danger.

Phantoms of a very different kind make sudden appearances in the German kitchens of Anna and Bernhard Blume (pp. 76-77). What habitats are these, we ask ourselves, where cups fly across the room and chairs upend themselves? We are in a strange locale here, where nothing has its place and imbalance reigns. Safer perhaps, are the mealtimes photographed by Robert Hammerstiel (pp. 78, 79); laid out for our inspection, we can invest these quiet tables with our own whimsy, our own imaginings. Hammerstiel gives us certain clues about the lives of those who hover out of the range of his camera – Frau Z likes to serve herself from a saucepan and her meal is dark and dour, while Frau H decorates the table to satisfy herself alone. But the information is partial and tantalising. Hammerstiel's photographs are puzzles for which there are no easy solutions; they provide the beginning of a story for which the denouement is subtly missing.

In the sophisticated homes of wealthy New Yorkers, a sidelong glance means as much as a shout. Tina Barney's family narratives are made with an acerbic eye, as she delineates the fine lines of relationship, looks closely and with irony at the hierarchies which inhabit domestica (pp. 80-81). Writing of Barney's photographs in the *New York Times*, Michael Brenson observed:

In all the works is sympathy for a way of life that promises a sense of family and a respect for privacy. In all the works there is also a feeling that beneath the clean, well-lighted surfaces are undercurrents of insecurity and competition in which everyone can drown.[19]

19.
Friends and Relations : Photographs by Tina Barney. Smithsonian Institution Press, Washington and London 1991

Entirely alien to this discreet comedy is Nick Waplington's story of the tenants of a Nottingham council house (pp. 82, 83). The lives of Janet, her partner and her children are played out on the edge. Damaged angels and bellicose madonnas enact the parts that society has cruelly written for them. Waplington's continuing series of

Sally Mann
The New Mothers
1989

Sally Mann
The Terrible Picture
1989

photographs are made on an epic scale, colours riot, figures swarm, and serendipity makes a manic chaos. While many commentators have seen these photographs as a swingeing condemnation of life in the Eighties, Waplington himself sees this extensive and ongoing documentary as:

> *a record of my time with the family. Documentary photographs often come with a big set of morals, but I'm not trying to make any kind of statement; the work is a record of the time I've spent with them. When I began the project, I'd seen pictures of housing estates, black and white photographs of the old school. The people in them looked like victims, and I wanted to show that they're not. They're not being beaten. These people are fighting back.*[20]

Nick Waplington was in his early twenties when he embarked on this series of photographs,[21] and he sees himself as intimately linked with Janet and her children. In a way, their story has become his story, and the divisions between the private and the public have been irrevocably blurred.

Carrie Mae Weems' highly staged domestic scenes are open to many interpretations (pp. 84, 85). One does not feel that they play out a specifically Black experience, rather that they are vignettes of family encounters, surreal and satirical. In succulent black and white, they transcend the documentary form which they seem at times to mimic, leaving us confused about the nature of 'the real'.

The group portraits of Thomas Struth (pp. 2-3, 86-87) and the Lafayette studios (pp. 75, 111) are separated by over sixty years of photographic and social history, but the stories which they tell are remarkably similar. In a recent interview with Benjamin Buchloh, Struth said of his family portraits:

> *These photographs originate in an intensive involvement in family photography which I had earlier as a student. Out of curiosity and historical interest, a curiosity to scrutinize stories, or to compare the stories that were told with photos, I always wondered if the stories were true, or whether the stories may be traced through pictures.*[22]

Struth's post-modernistic interest in narrative and the ambiguity of meaning stands at the centre of any study of these photographs.

> *This work* he insists *is primarily a collaboration, between these people and me.*[23] *... From the beginning, the idea of the portrait series was to make an exhibition. A space in which the people in the photos are very present, look into the lens and then indeed represent themselves, but at the same time pose questions.*[24]

While Struth's portraits are designed for gallery and museum spaces, the group photographs made by the Lafayette studios were destined for domestic use. But they too investigate ideas of family and group

20.
In conversation with the author 1994

21.
Some of these photographs have been published as *Living Room*, Cornerhouse, Manchester 1989

22.
From *Portraits: Thomas Struth*, Marian Goodman Gallery, New York 1990

23 & 24.
Ibid.

dynamics. A gathering of people, related by blood or by marriage pose together, and in doing so, describe most tellingly their relationships not only to each other, but to the still relatively new phenomenon of the camera. Some are more audacious than others when they gaze at this instrument, but all have their own messages to impart, their own tales to tell.

Every picture tells a story, and Bruce Gilden's photographs of children's parties in New York City have a particular narrative thread (pp. 88, 89). They are little tragedies, collisions between the demands of ritual and the accidents of real life. Tears are shed over the icing and confusion is evident. When we look at these photographs, from the distance of adulthood, we are conscious both of alienation and recognition.

The family forms the core of much great fiction. Jane Austen wove hers with delicacy around a myriad of group misunderstandings, and, many years later, the American short story writer Raymond Carver made agonizing statements about the misunderstandings and miseries of that place we call home. But, for all that, the family remains a kind of shrine at which we all worship, however covertly. Irish photographer Anthony Haughey and the adults and children of the Boorman family have both paid homage to this institution which impinges on our deepest feelings.

Haughey's series *Home* (1991-92) looks with a loving, yet still critical eye at his uncle's family living on a Dublin council estate (pp. 90, 91). His photographs are the story of lives severely limited by circumstance, but redeemed by some ineffable quality of faith or unity. Haughey prefixes his photo series with Article 41 of the Irish Constitution, which deals with the position of the family within the state. The repression which this Catholic country imposes on its citizens, spelt out in the laconic language of politics is all too clear. Haughey's *Home* shows one family attempting to live a modern life (Michael Jackson posters inhabit the same space as portraits of Christ and the Pope) within this archaic structure. In Haughey's pictures, the children of working-class Ireland are thin and chaotic, saved perhaps by love, justified by piety, and the victims of a terrible history.

The Boorman family, Terry, Nick, Astrid, Austin and Maxwell have told their own family story through a photographic diary which began in 1991 (pp. 92, 93).[25] Originally selected by a magazine to make a self-portrait of the life of an 'ordinary' family, their pictures went beyond an editorial concept to become a deep and enduring composite of life in the Nineties. Like all family photography, the

25.
The Boorman family were invited to photograph themselves for one year by the *Telegraph Magazine*

Boormans' story is our story too; their lives touch upon ours and become a touchstone for our own experience.

Narrative is a complex and sometimes baffling endeavour. Every story teller has a point of view, conveyed through a recounting of fact and event, but remaining partial and idiosyncratic. The photographers who have constructed these family stories have taken real lives as their starting points, but do not pretend objectivity. The families they have photographed have entered a public arena, giving us, the audience, an opportunity to observe, to make comment, to judge and compare. The intimacy of these narratives defies a concept of reportage, or universalism, or of humanism. They invoke ghosts, perhaps summon demons, or even perform the act of redemption.

Lafayette, Manchester studio
Mrs Bryde and her Three Children
3 May 1926
National Portrait Gallery
London

Anna and Bernhard Blume
Küchenkoller [*Kitchen Frenzy*]
1985 - 86
Kunstmuseum Düsseldorf
im Ehrenhof

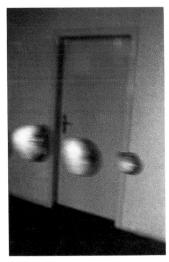

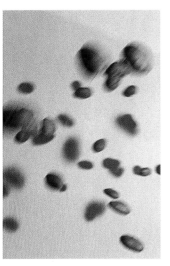

Robert F. Hammerstiel
from *Mittagsporträts*
[*Midday Portraits*]
1989-90

HERR UND FRAU B. UND KIND

Robert F. Hammerstiel
from *Mittagsporträts*
1989-90

HERR ST.

Tina Barney
Jill and Polly in the Bathroom
1987
Courtesy Janet Borden Inc.
New York

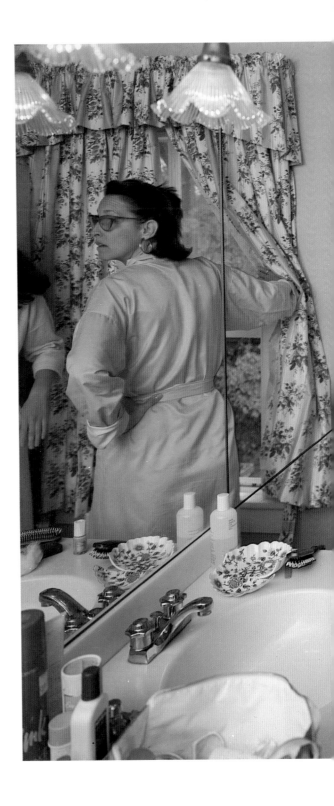

Carrie Mae Weems
Untitled
1990
Courtesy PPOW, New York

Previous pages:
Nick Waplington
from *Living Room*
1987-94

Carrie Mae Weems
Untitled
1990
Courtesy PPOW, New York

Thomas Struth
The Shimada Family,
Yamaguchi
1986
Courtesy Galerie Max Hetzler, Berlin

Bruce Gilden, from *Children's Birthday Parties* 1993

Anthony Haughey
from *Home*
1991-92
Two parts of a triptych

Terry, Nick, Austin and Maxwell in Tent

Terry in Sleeping Bag in Tent

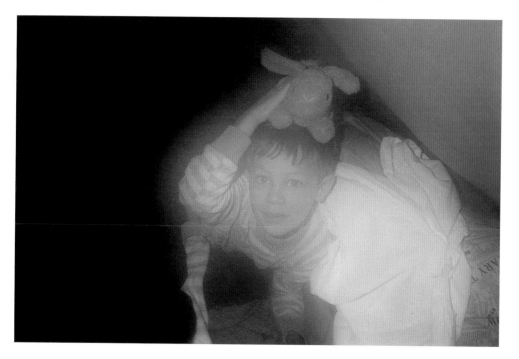

Astrid in Tent

In Memoriam

'The vast and terrible depth'
'Of course', he said.
'The inexhaustibility'.
'I understand'.
'The whole huge nameless thing'.
'Yes, absolutely'.
'The massive darkness'.
'Certainly, certainly'.
'The whole terrible endless hugeness'.
'I know exactly what you mean'.

Don Delillo, *White Noise*
[Viking Penguin Inc., London]
1984

In the western world, we have difficulties in dealing with death, and
its representation has become a taboo. Artists – like Joel Peter Witkin
and Andreas Serrano – have achieved a certain notoriety and a great
deal of fame by appearing to confront this problematic issue, while
at the same time, by their use of the grotesque and the horrible,
reinforcing popular notions of the gruesome nature of dead bodies.
The photographs included in this exhibition take a very different
stance – injured cadavers and dismembered body parts form no part
of this iconography. In the works included here, death is neither
objectified nor fetishised; instead it is represented as a symbol of
mourning, of a body lost but a spirit retained, a recognition of a rite
of passage and a central part of family life.

When 19th-century daguerreotypists photographed the dead
children of Victorian families, they acknowledged the fact and the
sight of infant mortality, and recognized the need for memorial. The
body of a dead child, seen through the pragmatic eyes of a society in
which infant death was an inevitable fact of everyday life, was neither
an obscenity nor an object of desire. Framed in the elaborate tracery
of gilt, enclosed in deep-toned leather or velvet, these photographs
took their place in family history (opposite).

Mari Mahr's photo piece *Between Ourselves* celebrates the past
and present, the living and the dead (pp. 96, 97). The work pays
homage to relationship and to lineage. Mari Mahr has written:

My mother's memory remains in myriads of things that surround me
– whether in some drawing pins I happen to be using or a hundred-
year-old tree I am passing by. Regardless of their scale, in reality,
all these things are of equal significance when lined up in my mind.
The symbol of an elegant woman represents my grandmother. I am
always looking through photographs of the 1920s and '30s taken in
artistic circles in Paris, hoping to find her in one of them – to visually

Albert J. Beals
New York City
Mother with her Dead Daughter
Posed in Painterly Convention
of the 'Sick Child'
*c.*1852
The Stanley B. Burns, M.D. Collection

Mari Mahr
Time for Sorrow 1991
from *Between Ourselves*
(detail opposite)

Overleaf:
Corinne Noordenbos
Alzheimers 2
Alzheimers 4
1993

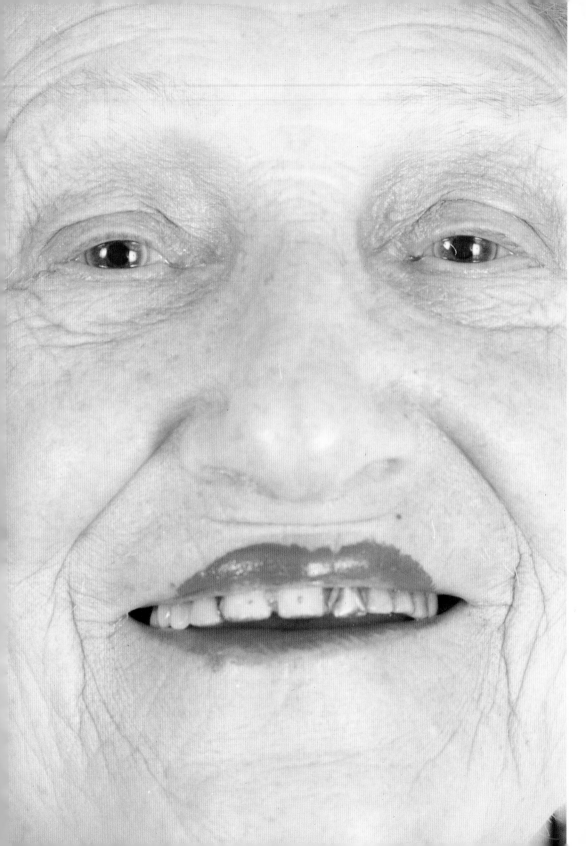

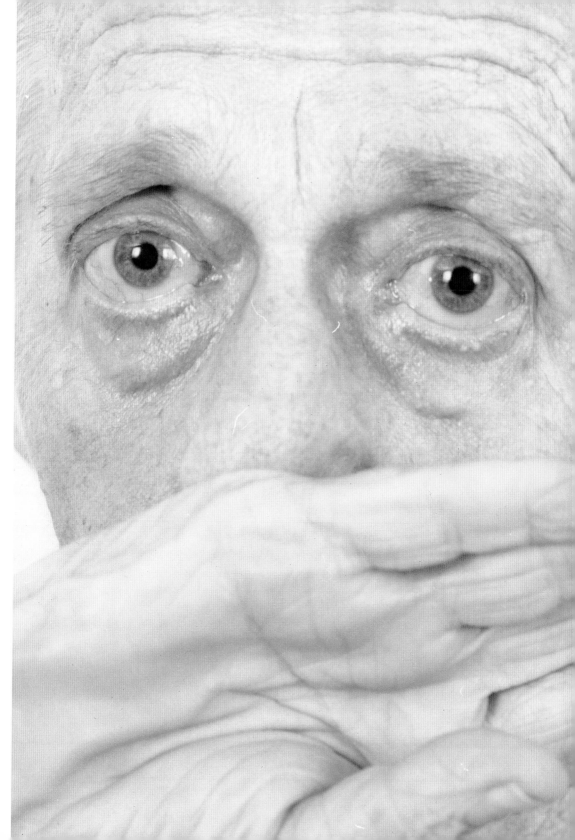

match all the stories I was told when I was young. Amongst all those
anonymous faces I can only find her friends . . . Hungarian painters,
writers and photographers.

As a child, living with her in the '50s, I concentrated only on small
details, for instance what were for me, her embarrassingly fancy shoes
(when everybody else was wearing tracksuits and trainers). I never
realised at the time her daring in rebelling against conformity.

In My Daughter, My Darling . . . *I have constructed a stage upon*
which to converse with my daughter. The stage (her vocation) is set
against a Chilean landscape (where I was born and a place of lifelong
concern to my mother). I feel I am here passing on to my daughter
all that has been passed on to me by my mother. This stage can
continue to be a place for such dialogue between us.[26]

26.
Unpublished papers,
Mari Mahr,
February 1994

Between Ourselves pays tribute not only to the dead, but to the
connections and the memories which continue after the physical fact.
It points out that elegy is necessary and that the past is always
apparent in the present.

Dutch photographer Corinne Noordenbos has made a stark and
painful series of portraits of men and women suffering from
Alzheimers disease, the condition from which her own mother died
(pp. 98, 99). Alzheimers, Noordenbos has recently observed:

will confront us increasingly. Already, ten percent of the elderly
suffer from the illness, nevertheless, a taboo surrounds it. People
would like to push any knowledge of this disease away, and forget
about the many sufferers who are now cooped up in homes.

They are no longer taken seriously. Even though we cannot
communicate directly, in the sense of 'speaking with them', one can
communicate in many other ways, and see *the full lives of interested*
people that lie behind. That is what I want to show in this work.[27]

27.
Unpublished papers,
Corinne Noordenbos
1994

In Noordenbos's series, the faces of these elderly people, lost in
the confusion of memory and sensibility which dementia brings, stare
out at the photographer, vestiges perhaps of their former selves, but
presences which cannot be denied.

When Liz Rideal's grandmother died in her nineties, Rideal
embarked on a photo-series which would act as a remembrance and
also confront issues of ageing (pp. 102-3). The bond between Rideal
and her grandmother was a strong one, and these photographs remind
us that the strength of such relationships does not end in death. There
is a suggestion of some spiritual continuity, an intimation of an
afterlife, all raised with obliqueness and inquiry. Rideal makes a
connection between life and death, and removes the taboo which
makes for absolute distinction between the two.

Irish photographer Tony O'Shea has a distinguished record as a

social documentarist. His photo-series on the illness and subsequent
death of his father, Con O'Shea, looks closely and with humility at
the debilitation of old age (pp. 104, 105). O'Shea is no cool observer
of another person's grief; the sorrow which echoes through these
photographs is his own. These are angry documents, as a son watches
the strong body of his father become inexorably enfeebled – they are
a statement of confusion and loss, made, one feels, with a sense of
utter desperation.

Everyone memorialises death in the family in different ways, and
each death is unique. Memorials stand as a concrete expression of the
way we feel about those who have disappeared from our lives.
Whether made of stone, or of film and paper, of language, or simply
kept in the heart, they are votive places, retained stubbornly against
the passage of time.

Overleaf:
Liz Rideal
Disappearing Act :
Marthe Callet (née Bailleul) 1896 - 1993
1993
four images of a work
in six parts

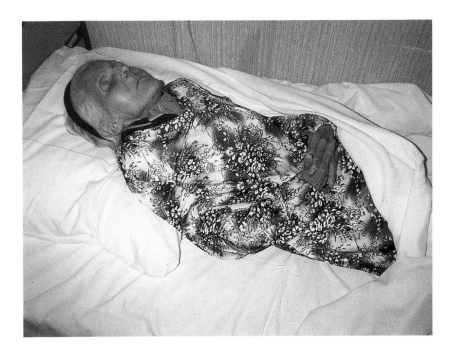

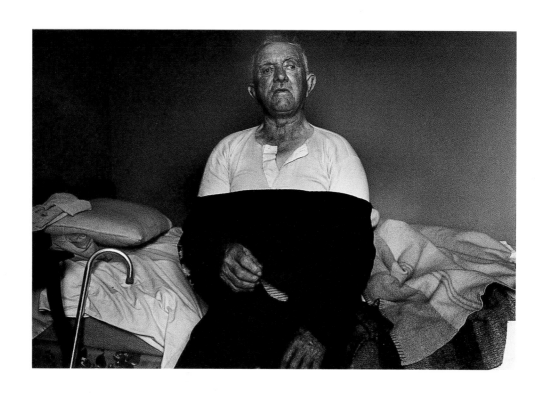

Tony O'Shea
This page and opposite:
from the series *Father*
1986-88

Endpiece:
Riddles and Conundrums

Family lives are full of contradictions, and family photography remains true to the ambiguities of real life. The decision whether to include Aki Yamamoto's work on abortion *De-Termination* (opposite) in this exhibition was a complicated one to make. Some would say that abortion was a negation of family life, and others insist that the decision whether or not to bear children should rest with women alone. It is an issue which society will continue to discuss. Abortion carries its own taboos, and Yamamoto's photo assemblage, so central to her own life, confronts our fears of the surgeon's forceps, the anaesthetist's needle, the patient's chair in a way which is immensely more powerful and suggestive than a piece of reportage could be. It is a cool, classic document, informed by terror.

Conundrums exist too in Jananne Al-Ani's exploration of the collision between family life and the facts of war (pp. 108-9). She uses photography to juxtapose views of her Iraqi homeland (employing war reportage, historical document and the family album) to create a composite picture which offers no explanations and no easy solutions to the dysfunction which comes not from within the family, but from the ambitions of politicians and the turmoil of war.

When the photographers employed by the Lafayette studios in the Twenties and Thirties photographed sisters, they also uncovered one of the riddles of family life (p. 111). Bound together by genealogy, and sometimes by little else, the bond between siblings is something which biology and society has imposed on individuals, and the strength of narcissism is nowhere more apparent. When a Lafayette photographer made a portrait of two sisters dressed to be bridesmaids in 1928 he seemed to sense a discomfort of relationship so subtle as to be almost invisible. Over thirty years later, in another country, Diane Arbus would make portraits which performed the same function.

In his series *Rich and Poor* (pp. 112, 113),[28] Jim Goldberg rejects the well versed opinions of family-watchers and asks family members to comment on the state of their lives and the relationships which form them. 'I feel like a piece of furniture' says one boy, and of her husband, a young woman observes sadly 'I wish that Stanley and I could like each other when we are together, but we don't'.

28.
Published by
Random House,
New York
1985

Aki Yamamoto
*Determination I
(Burden of Guilt)*
1993

Jananne Al-Ani
Untitled, May 1991

Goldberg's series both affirms and denies the power of documentary, contrasting appearances with reality and presenting a complex set of truths.

Family photography is a tendentious subject. Passing through this exhibition, you may not find a family who looks like yours, and nowhere is there one which exactly mirrors mine. The families who are represented here may well challenge the image which photographers have made of them, and, given another opportunity, those photographers may have chosen to do it differently. This essay began with a discussion of a painting by Gainsborough of a family whose stalwart elegance seemed to sum up what 'family' meant at the time. Some forty years earlier, William Hogarth painted *Marriage à la Mode : The Marriage Contract*, which showed a very different face of family life in 18th-century England. It showed a disreputable lawyer, a bored bridegroom, an anxious bride-to-be and two pompous fathers, who peer at the details of property and dowry in the marriage contract. The same country, much the same people, two portraits of the family, but the difference could not be more marked.

William Hogarth
*Marriage à la Mode :
The Marriage Contract*
*c.*1742-44
Reproduced by courtesy of
the Trustees, The National Gallery
London

Lafayette, Manchester studio
*Two Bridesmaids at the Wedding
of Geoffrey Kemp Bourne
and Agnes Evelyn Thompson*
11 July 1928
National Portrait Gallery
London

Jim Goldberg
Untitled 1979
opposite:
Untitled 1981
from the series *Rich and Poor* 1977-84

I LOVE DAVID. BUT HE IS TO
fragile for A Rough fATHER LiKE
ME

Terry J Benke

My wife is Acceptable.
Our relationship is satisfactory.
Edgar G.

Edgar looks splendid here. His power and
strength of character come through. He is a
very private person who is not demonstrative
of his affection; that has never made me
unhappy. I accept him as he is.
    We are totally devoted to each other.
                    Regina Goldstine
Dear Jim:
    May you be as lucky in marriage!

Earlier in this text, Mark Haworth-Booth pondered over the definition of 'ordinary', and perhaps we too should spare a little time for reflection on this most bizarre of categorizations. In the Fifties and Sixties, the artist Harry Wingfield provided the illustrations for a number of Ladybird children's books. In his drawings (which have all the exactitude of photographs), we are confronted by the quintessence of normality. But examine these books with those who are now in their forties, and whose childhoods were in some subtle ways formed by them, and no-one can quite remember having families as 'ordinary' as these (pp. 10, 127).

Who's Looking at the Family? is not for those who are looking to discover what 'family' means. It is rather an exploration of what some families looked like at a certain time, in particular places, seen through different sets of eyes. It explores the notion of looking, examines ideas of narrative and ponders on the uses of this diverse and problematic medium of photography. In years to come, some curious person may come across the photographs assembled here and ask themselves 'But was it really like this?'. The answer to this question is 'of course', 'sometimes', 'maybe', 'never', or 'perhaps'.

. . . and then there is no end to it, words, words, words.
At best and most they are perhaps in memoriam, evocations,
conjurations, incantations, emanations, shimmering,
iridescent flares in the sky of darkness, a just still feasible tact,
indiscretions, perhaps forgivable . . .
R.D. Laing:
The Politics of Experience and the Bird of Paradise.
[Penguin Books, Harmondsworth]
1967

Martin Parr
Love Cubes 1972, key to pairs
see pp. 16 - 17

Biographical Notes

Selected recent exhibitions and publications only are listed

Jananne Al-Ani
pp. 108–9

Born, Kirkuk, Iraq, 1966. Studied at Byam Shaw School of Art, London, 1986–89. Lives and works in London.
Recent exhibitions include:
1989 and 1990: *Whitechapel Open*, Whitechapel Art Gallery, London. 1991: *Guernica Revisited*, Kufa Gallery, London; *Contact*, South Bank Centre, London (prizewinner); *Sign of the Times*, Camerawork, London. 1992: *Whitechapel Open*, Whitechapel Art Gallery, London; *Fine material for a dream . . .? A Reappraisal of Orientalism*, Harris Museum and Art Gallery, Preston, and tour to Ferens Museum and Art Gallery, Hull, and Oldham Art Gallery. 1993: *Declarations of War: Contemporary art from the collection of the Imperial War Museum*, Kettle's Yard, Cambridge; *No More Heroes Anymore*, Royal Scottish Academy, Edinburgh.
Selected publications:
Fine material for a dream . . .? A Reappraisal of Orientalism, catalogue, Harris Museum and Art Gallery, Preston, 1992.

Gerry Anderson
pp. 7, 34, 35

Born, London, 1929. Following a background in the British film industry, a move into television production in the late 1950s led to devising and producing some of the most popular and internationally acclaimed television fantasy series in the history of television. State-of-the-art technical sophistication became an Anderson trademark in both puppet and live action projects. Lives in Henley-on-Thames.
Television credits include:
1962: *Fireball XL5*. 1963: *Stingray*. 1965: *Thunderbirds*. 1967: *Captain Scarlet and The Mysterons*. 1968: *Joe 90*. 1970: *U.F.O.* 1975: *Space: 1999*. 1983: *Terrahawks*. 1985: *Dick Spanner P.I.* 1994: *Space Police*.
Film credits include:
1966: *Thunderbirds Are Go*. 1968: *Thunderbird 6*. 1969: *Doppelganger (Journey to the Far Side of the Sun)*.
Numerous television tie-in comics and annuals including:
1965–1970's: *TV21* introduced innovative front page layout using photographs accompanied by newspaper-style headlines and captions. 1967: *Candy and Andy*, the first photo-story comic for the nursery market.

Tina Barney
pp. 80–81

Born, New York, 1945. Studied at Sun Valley Center for Arts and Humanities, 1976–79. Lives and works in Rhode Island.
Recent exhibitions include:
1990: Museum of Modern Art, New York (solo); *The Art of Photography 1839–1989*, The Seibu Museum of Art, Tokyo; Cleveland Center for Contemporary Art, Ohio (solo). 1991: *Blood Relatives*, Milwaukee Art Museum; International Museum of Photography at George Eastman House, Rochester, NY (solo); *Pleasures and Terrors of Domestic Comfort*, Museum of Modern Art, New York. 1993: Janet Borden, Inc., New York (solo); *In and Out of Place*, Museum of Fine Arts, Boston; *Commodity Image*, International Center of Photography, New York; *In Camera*, Museum of New Mexico, Santa Fe.
Collections include:
Baltimore Art Museum; Museum of Fine Arts, Boston; Museum of Modern Art, New York; National Museum of American Art, Washington DC; Yale University Art Gallery, New Haven.
Selected publications:
Swimmers, collaborative book with Tina Howe, Friends of the Whitney Museum Library, New York, 1991; *Pleasures and Terrors of Domestic Comfort*, catalogue, Museum of Modern Art, New York, 1991; *Friends and Relations*, monograph, Smithsonian Institution Press, Washington DC, 1992.

Richard Billingham
pp. 45, 46, 47

Born, Birmingham, 1970. Studied at Bournville College and Sunderland University (Fine Art). Lives and works in Sunderland.

Anna and Bernhard Blume
pp. 76–77

Anna Blume: born, Bork, Germany, 1937. Studied at Staatlichen Kunstakademie, Düsseldorf.
Bernhard Blume: born, Dortmund, Germany, 1937. Studied at Staatlichen Kunstakademie, Düsseldorf and University of Cologne. Anna and Bernhard Blume live and work in Cologne.
Recent exhibitions include:
1989: Museum of Modern Art, New York (joint). 1990: National Museum of Modern Art, Tokyo; Centro d'arte Santa Monica, Barcelona. 1991: Margarete Roeder Gallery, New York (joint); Kunstverein Ruhr e. V., Essen (joint); Galerie Ak, Frankfurt (joint); Kunstmuseum Düsseldorf. 1992: Grosse Deichtorhalle, Hamburg (joint); Walker Art Center, Minneapolis; Dallas Museum of Art, Texas; Solomon R. Guggenheim Museum, New York.

1993: Wiener Sezession, Vienna (joint); Landesmuseum Münster (joint).

Selected publications:
Anna & Bernhard Blume : Grossfotoserien 1985–1990, monograph, Rheinland-Verlag, Cologne, 1992.

The Boorman Family
pp. 92, 93

Comprises five members:
Nick Boorman, born 1953; Terry Boorman, born 1954; Astrid Boorman, born 1985; Austin Boorman, born 1987; Maxwell Boorman, born 1989. The Boormans live in Middlesex.

The Boorman family took approximately 20,000 photographs of their daily lives between May 1991 and August 1992 for an article published in the *Telegraph Magazine* in October 1992. A selection of these photographs were exhibited in 1993, at Impressions Gallery, York and tour.

The photographs on show at Barbican Art Gallery are some of those taken for the *Telegraph Magazine*, but also include photographs taken more recently.

Florence Chevallier
pp. 22, 23

Born, Casablanca, Morocco, 1955. Studied at the Institute of Theatrical Studies, Paris. Founder member of Groupe Noir Limite, 1986-93. Lives and works in Saint-Saëns, France.

Recent exhibitions include:
1980: *Selfportraits*, Pompidou Centre, Paris. 1988: International Festival of Photography, Montreal; *Noir Limite : Corps à Corps* (censored exhibition), Maison de la Culture, Bourges. 1989: FNAC, Palais de Tokyo, Paris. 1990: *Photographie actuelle*, Gulbenkian Foundation, Lisbon. 1991: *Découvertes*, Collection de la Bibliothèque Nationale, Grand-Palais, Paris; *Contemporary French Photography*, International Center of Photography, New York and tour. 1993: *Le Bonheur*, Galerie Barbier-Beltz, Paris and tour (solo).

Recent commissions include:
Conseil Général des Côtes d'Armor, *Patrimoine* 1990. Grant from FIACRE, Ministère de la Culture, 1991.

Collections include:
Bibliothèque Nationale, Paris; Fonds National d'Art Contemporain, Paris; Musée de la Photographie, Charleroi.

Selected publications:
Noir Limite : Corps à Corps, catalogue, Photo and Co., 1987; *Les Cahiers de la Photographie : 20 ans de Photographie Créative en France*, G.Mora, 1989; *Noir Limite la Mort*, Photo and Co., 1991; *Le Bonheur*, La Différence, Paris, 1993.

Linda Duvall
pp. 32–33

Born, Newington, Ontario, 1950. Studied at Carleton University, Ottawa (BA English and Sociology) 1972; Queen's University, Kingston (B.Ed Education) 1974; Ontario College of Art, Toronto (AOCA General Studies/ Photography) 1980; University of Michigan, Ann Arbor (MFA Interdisciplinary Studies) 1994. Lives and works in Saskatoon, Saskatchewan, and Ann Arbor, Michigan.

Recent exhibitions include:
1990: *Turtle Soup*, Cornwall Regional Art Gallery, Ontario (solo); *Women's Friend*, Concordia Art Gallery, Montreal, Quebec. 1992: *Paperbacked/Paperbound*, Blackwood Gallery, Erindale College, Toronto. 1993: *Photo Re :Union – Processing History*, Hamilton Artists' Inc., Hamilton, Ontario; *Bookworks at AKA*, AKA Artists' Centre, Saskatoon, Saskatchewan; *Women and Madness : The Social Construction of Identity*, Tucson, Arizona; *Echo*, Rackham Galleries, University of Michigan, Ann Arbor (solo). 1994: *Examining Room*, Ceres Gallery, New York.

Selected publications:
Quandary : Recent Work by Linda Duvall, catalogue, Art Gallery of Hamilton, Ontario, 1988; *Linda Duvall : Installation*, catalogue, Lindsay Gallery, Ontario, 1990.

Bruce Gilden
pp. 88, 89

Born, New York, 1946. Lives and works in New York.
Recent exhibitions include:
1989: Bibliothèque Nationale, Paris. 1990: Agathe Gaillard Gallery, Paris. 1992: Fotographie Forum, Frankfurt (solo); The Chrysler Museum, Norfolk, Virginia (solo). 1993: *Recent Acquisitions*, Museum of Modern Art, New York; Special Photographers Company, London (solo); Musée de l'Elysée, Lausanne (solo).

Awards include:
National Endowment for the Arts Photographer's Fellowship 1980, 1984, 1992. Artist's Fellowship Award, New York Foundation for the Arts, 1979, 1992. Mission Photographique Transmanche, Centre Régional de la Photographie, Nord Pas-de-Calais, 1993.

Collections include:
Paris Audiovisual, Paris; Moderna Museet, Stockholm; Musée de la Photographie, Belgium; Museum of Fine Arts, Houston, Texas; Museum of Modern Art, New York; Victoria and Albert Museum, London.

Selected publications:
Opus Small Portfolios of Great Photographs, Issue no.1, 1990; *Bruce Gilden, The Small Haiti Portfolio* (limited edition), Helsinki, 1990; *Facing New York : Photographs by Bruce Gilden*, Cornerhouse Publications, Manchester, 1992; *Aperture* magazine, no.126 (Haiti issue, portfolio), New York, 1992; Mission Photographique Transmanche Cahier no.13, 1994; *Bleus*, Centre Régional de la Photographie, Nord Pas-de-Calais, 1994.

Jim Goldberg
pp. 112, 113

Born, New Haven, Mass., 1953. Studied at Western
Washington University, Bellingham (BA Photography and
Education), 1975, and San Francisco Art Institute (MFA
Photography) 1979. Lives and works in San Francisco.
Recent exhibitions include:
1989: *Capp Street Project*, San Francisco (solo). 1990:
Washington Project for the Arts, Washington DC (solo); *Art
at the Anchorage*, Creative Time, New York (solo). 1991:
Art in General, New York (solo). 1995: *Raised by Wolves*,
Corcoran Gallery of Art, Washington DC; Addison
Gallery of American Art, Boston; and Museum für
Gestaltung, Zurich.
Recent awards include:
Guggenheim Fellowship, 1985. National Endowment for
the Arts Fellowship, 1990. California Arts Council
Fellowship, 1990. Glen Eagles Foundation Grant, 1992.
Collections include:
Boston Museum of Fine Arts; Library of Congress,
Washington DC; Museum of Modern Art, New York; San
Francisco Museum of Modern Art; Seattle Art Museum;
Smithsonian Institution, Washington DC.
Selected publications:
Rich & Poor, Random House, New York, 1985; *Raised by
Wolves*, Scalo Publications, Zurich, 1994.

Robert F. Hammerstiel
pp. 78, 79

Born, Pottschach, Austria, 1957.
Studied at University of Vienna (Literature) 1976–83 and
Hochschule für angewandte Kunst (Photography) 1979–
83. Lives and works in Vienna.
Recent exhibitions include:
1991: Mai de la photo, Reims (solo); Wolfgang Gurlitt
Museum, Linz (solo); Museum für Photographie,
Braunschweig (solo); Heidelberger Kunstverein,
Heidelberg (solo); Akhnaton Gallery, Cairo (solo). 1992:
Museet for Fotokunst, Odense (solo). 1993: Salzburger
Landesmuseum Rupertinum, Salzburg (solo);
Departemento de Fotografia, Cordoba (solo). 1994: LA
Gallery, Frankfurt/Main (solo); Focke Museum, Bremen
(solo).
Recent commissions and awards include:
Landesatelier Salzburg, Salzburger Landesmuseum,
Salzburg, 1990. Workshop Gieraltow, Foto Medium Art
Galeria, Wroclaw, 1991. *Das andere Mittelalter*, Kunst
Halle Krems, 1992. Romstipendium, Bundesministerium
für Kultur, Austria, 1993.
Selected Publications:
Der Stande der Dinge, monograph, Linz, 1991; *Im Bilde v.
obraze. Aktuelle Fotografie aus Österreich*, catalogue,
Vienna, 1991; *European Photography Awards*, catalogue,
Göttingen, 1992.

Anthony Haughey
pp. 90, 91

Born, Keady, Armagh, Northern Ireland, 1963.
Studied at West Surrey College of Art and Design,
Farnham, 1988–91. Lives and works in Dublin.
Recent exhibitions include:
1992: *Home*, Irish Gallery of Photography, Dublin and
tour (solo); *Current Account*, Mai de la photo, Reims;
On the Face of Europe, Derby Photography Festival. 1993:
Documentary Dilemmas, British Council touring exhibition.
Recent awards include:
ICI International Photography Awards (runner-up),
National Portrait Gallery, London, and National Museum
of Photography, Film and Television, Bradford, 1992.
European Photography Awards, Hamburg, 1993.

John Heatley
pp. 63

Born, Preston, 1961. Since 1980 has been a police constable
in the Lancashire Constabulary, completing an Initial
Scenes of Crime course in 1983. Reserve Scenes of Crime
Officer in the Chorley area 1983–85; transferred to Preston
in 1986 as Scenes of Crime Officer. From 1991 based at the
Headquarters Scenes of Crime Unit at Hutton, Preston,
where he provides county wide cover. Also lectures on
scenes of crime matters.

Alexander Honory
pp. 36–37 & cover

Born, Esslingen, Germany, 1957. Studied at Film school,
Łódź, Poland, 1980–83. Founded the Private Institute of
Contemporary Family Photography, 1979. Lives and
works in Cologne.
Recent exhibitions include:
1990: Galerie Wschodnia, Łódź (solo); Galerie Potocka,
Kraków (solo); *Construction in Process, Back in Łódź*,
Łódź. 1991: PS1, New York; *The Circle of Wschodnia*, The
Centre of Contemporary Art, Warsaw; The 4th Fukui
International Video Biennale, Fukui. 1992: Städtische
Galerie Nordhorn (solo); *Łódz Avant Garde 1970–1992*,
Grohmann Palace, Łódź. 1993: Münchner Stadtmuseum,
Fotomuseum, Munich (solo); Het Apollohuis, Eindhoven
(solo); KMSK, ICC, Antwerp (solo); Galerie
Theuretzbacher, Vienna (solo); *Privat*, Kunst-Werke
Berlin, Berlin; Galerie Theuretzbacher, Vienna (solo).
1994: Galerie Potocha, Kraków (solo).
Selected publications:
Das Gefundene Bild, Nordhorn, 1992; *APEX* no.15,
Cologne, 1992; *FAZ-Magazin*, no.681, March 1993; *Das
Gefundene Bild*, KMSK/ICC, Antwerp, 1993; *Raum mit
Photos*, Hake Verlag, Cologne, 1993.

Ouka Lele (Barbara Allende)

pp. 54, 55

Born, Madrid, 1957. Self-taught. Lives and works in Madrid.

Recent exhibitions include:
1990: ARCO '90, Galería Moriarty, Madrid; *Spanish Fine Art Photography*, Special Photographers Company, London; *D'un Art, L'Autre. Mise en Scène*, Musées de Marseille. 1991: *Cuatro Direcciones: 20 Años de Fotografía Contemporánea Española 1970–1990*, Centro de Arte Reina Sofia, Madrid. 1992: *Almediterranea '92*, Exposición Universal de Sevilla, Expo 92, Seville; *Ouka Lele*, Special Photographers Company, London. 1993: *Ouka Lele: Fotografías y Pinturas*, Galeria Masha Prieto, Madrid.

Recent commissions include:
Volaverunt, Fundació 'la Caixa', Barcelona; Fencis, Museu d'Art Contemporani, Ibiza.

Selected publications:
Naturaleza viva: Naturaleza muerta, Ediciones Arnao, 1986; *Deixeu el balcó obert: La fotografia en l'art contemporani espanyol*, Fundació 'la Caixa', Barcelona, 1992.

Susan Lipper

pp. 68, 69

Born, New York, 1953. Studied at Yale University (MFA Photography) 1981–83. Lives and works in New York.

Recent exhibitions include:
1986: *Recent Acquisitions*, National Portrait Gallery, London. 1987: *Current Works 87*, Kansas City Art Institute, Missouri. 1989: Midtown Y Photography Gallery, New York (solo). 1990: Fordham University, Duane Gallery, New York (solo). 1991: Chenango County Arts Council, Norwich, NY (with Andrea Modica). 1994: *Grapevine Hollow*, The Photographers' Gallery, London (solo); *In the Hollows, Appalachian Perspectives: Susan Lipper and Wendy Ewald*, pARTs Gallery, Minneapolis; *Grapevine*, Arnolfini, Bristol (solo).

Collections include:
Bibliothèque Nationale, Paris; Metropolitan Museum of Art, New York; National Portrait Gallery, London.

Selected publications:
Graduate Photography at Yale, Yale School of Art, New Haven, 1983; *Grapevine: Photographs by Susan Lipper*, monograph, Cornerhouse Publications, Manchester, 1994.

Katrina Lithgow

pp. 50, 51

Born, Glasgow, 1968. Studied at Bath College of Higher Education 1987–88; West Surrey College of Art & Design, (BA Audio Visual Studies) 1988–91, and Royal College of Art, London (MA Photography) 1993–95. Lives and works in London.

Recent exhibitions include:
1991: *Whitworth Young Contemporaries*, Manchester. 1992: The Photographers' Gallery, London and tour (solo).

Selected publications:
A Stuggy Pren, project with Ivor Cutler, Littlewood ARC Publications, 1994.

Doug Luke

pp. 7, 34, 35

Born, Sunbury-on-Thames, 1929. Trained at the printing department of Shepperton Film Studios, late 1940s. Lives in Middlesex.

Head printer, stills department, Shepperton Studios, 1960–63. Freelance portrait and stills photographer in film, television and advertising, 1963–91.

Commissions include:
1965–early 1970s: Gerry Anderson's *TV 21* productions including *Thunderbirds, Captain Scarlet, U.F.O.* and *Candy and Andy*.

Mari Mahr

pp. 96–97

Born, Santiago, Chile, 1941. Studied at the School of Journalism, Budapest, and Polytechnic of Central London (BA Photographic Arts). Lives and works in London.

Recent exhibitions include:
1989: *Through the Looking Glass: British Photography 1945–89*, Barbican Art Gallery, London. 1990: *Fotofest*, Houston, Texas (solo); *Primavera Fotográfica*, Barcelona and tour (solo). 1991: Les Ateliers Nadar, Marseille (solo); *De Vierde Wand: Photography as Theatre*, Amsterdam. 1992: Portfolio Gallery, Edinburgh (solo). Mai de la photo, Reims; *2. Internationale Foto-Triennale*, Esslingen. 1993: *Moving into View*, South Bank Centre, London. 1994: Montage Gallery, Derby (solo).

Awards include:
Fox Talbot Award, National Museum of Photography, Film & Television, Bradford, 1989.

Collections include:
Arts Council of England, London; The British Council, London; Scottish Art Gallery and Museum, Glasgow; Victoria and Albert Museum, London.

Selected publications:
A Few Days in Geneva, Travelling Light, London, 1988; *Isolated Incidents*, The Photographers' Gallery, London, 1989; *Through the Looking Glass: British Photography 1945–89*, catalogue, Barbican Art Gallery, London, 1989.

Sally Mann

pp. 71, 72

Born, Lexington, Virginia, 1951. Studied at Hollins College (BA and MA Writing) 1975; Praestegaard Film School (Photography) 1971; Aegean School of Fine Arts, 1972; Apeiron, 1973 and Ansel Adams Yosemite Workshop, 1973. Lives and works in Lexington, Virginia.

Recent exhibitions include:
1991: *Pleasures and Terrors of Domestic Comfort*, Museum of Modern Art, New York; *Biennial Exhibition*, Whitney Museum of American Art, New York. 1992: *Immediate Family*, Houk Friedman, New York, and Institute of Contemporary Art, Philadelphia (solo). 1993: *Still Time*, Museum of Contemporary Photography, Chicago (solo); *Elegant Intimacy*, Retretti Museum, Finland.

Recent awards include:
John Simon Guggenheim Foundation Fellowship, 1987. Artists in the Visual Arts Fellowship, 1989. National Endowment for the Arts Individual Artist Fellowship, 1982, 1988, 1992.

Collections include:

Metropolitan Museum of Art, New York; Museum of Modern Art, New York; San Francisco Museum of Art; Metropolitan Museum of Art, Tokyo; Whitney Museum of American Art, New York.
Selected publications:
At Twelve, Portraits of Young Women, monograph, Aperture Foundation Inc., New York, 1988; *Pleasures and Terrors of Domestic Comfort*, catalogue, Museum of Modern Art, New York, 1991; *Immediate Family*, monograph, Aperture Foundation Inc., New York, 1992; *Still Time*, catalogue, Aperture Foundation Inc., New York, 1994.

Corinne Noordenbos
pp. 98, 99

Born, Amsterdam. Studied at the Rietveld Academy, Amsterdam, 1968–73 and Royal Academy of Art, Amsterdam, 1977–80. Lives and works in Amsterdam.
Recent exhibitions include:
1989: *Foto '89*, Nieuwe Kerk, Amsterdam. 1990: Kunstmanifestatie A-Kerk, Groningen; *'Dubbeldruk' in de manifestatie 'Noorderlicht'*, Groningen. 1991: *De vorm van Nederland*, Stedelijk Museum, Amsterdam. 1992: *Kijkdozen op de Dam*, De Moor, Amsterdam.
Collections include:
Centre for Photography, Limburg, and the Dutch National Collection of Visual Art.

Tony O'Shea
pp. 104, 105

Born, Valentia Island, Co. Kerry, Ireland, 1947. Studied at University College, Dublin (BA Philosophy and English Literature) 1972. Began photographing professionally in 1981. Lives and works in Dublin.
Recent exhibitions include:
1987: *The Border*, Monaghan Arts Festival (solo). 1990: *Dubliners*, Gallery of Photography, Dublin (solo). 1991: *Europe . . . On the Dark Side of the Stars*, Arles Festival. 1992: *Premier Photo*, Galerie du Jour Agnès B, Paris.
Selected publications:
Walking along the Border (with Colm Tóibin), MacDonald Queen Anne Press, London, 1987; *Dubliners* (with Colm Tóibin), MacDonald, London, 1990; *Europe . . . On the Dark Side of the Stars*, Secours Populaire Français, Paris, 1991; *Premier Photo*, catalogue, Galerie du Jour Agnès B, Paris, 1992.

Martin Parr
pp. 16–17, 115

Born, Epsom, Surrey, 1952. Studied at Manchester Polytechnic (Photography) 1970–73. Associate member of Magnum agency. Lives and works in Bristol.
Recent exhibitions include:
1986: *The Last Resort*, Serpentine Gallery, London and tour (solo). 1989: *The Cost of Living*, Royal Photographic Society, Bath and tour (solo); *Through the Looking Glass : British Photography 1945–1989*, Barbican Art Gallery, London; *The Art of Photography*, Royal Academy, London. 1991: *British Photography from the Thatcher Years*, Museum of Modern Art, New York. 1992: *Signs of the Times*, Janet Borden, Inc., New York and Arles festival (solo). 1993: *Photographs from the Real World*,

Lilliehammer Art Museum, Norway; *Bored Couples*, Galerie du Jour Agnès B, Paris (solo); *Home and Abroad*, Watershed Gallery, Bristol and tour (solo).
Collections include:
Arts Council of England, London; Australian National Gallery, Canberra; Getty Museum, Malibu; Museum for Fotokunst, Odense; Museum of Modern Art, New York; Museum of Modern Art, Tokyo; Victoria and Albert Museum, London.
Selected publications:
The Last Resort, Promenade Press, Merseyside, 1986; *The Cost of Living*, catalogue, Cornerhouse Publications, Manchester, 1989; *Through the Looking Glass : British Photography 1945–89*, catalogue, Barbican Art Gallery, London, 1989; *Signs of the Times*, catalogue, Cornerhouse Publications, Manchester, 1992; *Bored Couples*, catalogue, Galerie du Jour Agnès B, Paris, 1993; *Home and Abroad*, catalogue, Jonathan Cape, London, 1993. *From A to B*, BBC Books, London, 1994.

Paul Reas
pp. 39, 40

Born, Bradford, 1955. Studied at Newport College of Art, 1982–84. Lives and works in Lancaster.
Recent exhibitions include:
1988: *I Can Help*, The Photographers' Gallery, London and tour (solo); Fotobienal, Vigo (solo). 1989: *Through the Looking Glass : British Photography 1945–1989*, Barbican Art Gallery, London; Olympus Gallery, Amsterdam (solo); *Condemned to Making Sense*, Perspektief Gallery, Rotterdam; Fotobienale, Enschede. 1990: *Vigo Visions*, Vigo; *Heritage Image and History*, Cornerhouse, Manchester and tour. 1992: *Arles Rencontre*, Arles; *ICI Awards*, National Portrait Gallery, London and tour. 1993: *Positive Lives*, The Photographers' Gallery, London and tour; *Documentary Dilemmas*, British Council touring exhibition; *Flogging a Dead Horse*, The Photographers' Gallery, London and tour (solo); Cornerhouse, Manchester (solo).
Recent awards and commissions include:
Arts Council of Great Britain Publication Award, 1992. ICI Fox Talbot Award nominee, 1992. The Andrew Sproxton Memorial Fund Award, 1993.
Collections include:
The British Council, London; Fotobienal, Vigo; Impressions Gallery, York; National Museum of Photography, Film & Television, Bradford; Welsh Arts Council.
Selected publications:
Towards a Bigger Picture : British Photography, Aperture Foundation Inc., New York, 1988; *I Can Help*, catalogue, Cornerhouse Publications, Manchester, 1988; *Through the Looking Glass : British Photography 1945–89*, catalogue, Barbican Art Gallery, London, 1989; *Image and History*, Impressions Gallery, York, 1990; *Vigo Visions*, catalogue, Vigo IV Fotobienal, Spain, 1990; *ICI Fox Talbot Awards*, catalogue, National Museum of Photography, Film & Television, Bradford, 1992; *Documentary Dilemmas*, catalogue, British Council Publication, 1993; *Positive Lives*, catalogue, Cassel Books, 1993; *Flogging a Dead Horse*, catalogue, Cornerhouse Publications, Manchester, 1993.

Liz Rideal
pp. 102–3

Born, UK, 1954. Studied at Brighton Polytechnic, 1972–73; Exeter College of Art and Design and Exeter University, 1973–76; Exeter University, 1977–78. Lives and works in London.
Recent exhibitions include:
1990: *A New Necessity*, First Tyne International Garden Festival and Laing Art Gallery, Newcastle-upon-Tyne; *Fairy Queen*, The Photographers' Gallery, London (solo); Orchard Gallery, Derry, N. Ireland (solo). 1991: Vancouver Art Gallery (solo); Portfolio Gallery, Edinburgh (solo). 1992: Royal Photographic Society, Bath (solo); Spacex Gallery, Exeter (solo). 1993: '*A mes beaux yeux' : Auto-portraits contemporains*, Espace Lyonnais d'Art Contemporain, Lyon.
Recent commissions include:
New British Library, London, 1989. Illustrations to *Lusus Naturae*, Circle Press, 1990. The Ivy Restaurant, West Street, London WC2, 1990.
Collections include:
Arts Council of England, London; Bibliothèque Nationale, Paris; National Portrait Gallery, London; Vancouver Art Gallery; Washington Library of Congress, Washington DC.
Selected publications:
A New Necessity, Tyne International, Newcastle-upon-Tyne, 1990; *Liz Rideal : Photobooth Collages*, Circle Press, London, 1990; *Lusus Naturae*, Circle Press, London, 1990; *Auto-portraits contemporains*, *Here's looking at me*, Espace Lynnais d'Art Contemporain, Ville de Lyon, 1993; *Facing the Page : British Artist's Books*, Estamp, London, 1993.

Thomas Ruff
pp. 64, 65, 67

Born, Zell am Harmersbach, Germany, 1958. Studied at the Staatlichen Kunstakademie, Düsseldorf. Lives and works in Düsseldorf.
Recent exhibitions include:
1990: *Magasin*, Centre National d'Art Contemporain de Grenoble (solo); Verein Kunsthalle Zürich (solo); *To be or not to be*, Centre d'Art de Santa Monica, Barcelona. 1991: Kunstverein, Bonn and tour (solo). 1992: *Qui, Quoi, Où*, Musée d'Art Moderne de la Ville de Paris; *Photography in Contemporary German Art : 1960 to the present*, Walker Art Center, Minneapolis and tour. 1993: *Konstruktion. Zitat – Kollektive Bilder in der Fotografie*, Sprengel Museum, Hannover; *Photographs from the Real World*, Lilliehammer Art Museum, Norway and tour; *Distanz und Nähe*, Neue Nationalgalerie, Berlin and tour.
Selected publications:
Photographs from the Real World, catalogue, Lilliehammer Art Museum, Norway, 1993; *Distanz und Nähe*, catalogue, Neue Nationalgalerie, Berlin, 1993.

Joachim Schmid
pp. 20–21

Born, Balingen, Germany, 1955. Studied at the Hochschule der Künste Berlin (Visual Communication) 1976–81. Lives and works in Berlin.
Recent exhibitions include:
1990: *Meesterwerken en andere Beelden*, Perspektief, Rotterdam (solo). 1991: *Erste allgemeine Altfotosammlung*, Bilderdienst, Berlin (solo); *Des Vessies et des Lanternes : Curiosités photographiques*, Botanique, Brussels and tour. 1992: *Cannibal Eyes*, MIT List Visual Arts Center, Cambridge, Massachusetts. 1993: *Joachim Schmid*, Blue Sky, Portland, Oregon (solo); *Art Addicts Anonymous : Berlin*, Bilderdienst, Berlin and tour (solo); *Within Memory*, Montage 93, Rochester, NY and tour; *Taking Snapshots : Amateur Photography in Germany from 1900 to the Present*, Queen's Hall, Edinburgh and tour (solo); *Retratos anónimos*, Museu da Imagem e do Som, São Paulo (solo).
Collections include:
Berlinische Galerie, Berlin; Bibliothèque Nationale, Paris; Museum Folkwang, Essen; Fotomuseum im Münchner Stadtmuseum, Munich.
Selected publications:
Cannibal Eyes, catalogue, MIT List Visual Arts Center, Cambridge, Massachusetts, 1992; *Taking Snapshots : Amateur Photography in Germany from 1900 to the Present*, catalogue, Institut für Auslandsbeziehungen, Berlin, 1993.

Margriet Smulders
pp. 52, 53

Born, Bussum, The Netherlands, 1955. Studied at K. University of Nijmegen (Psychology) 1975–83; Academy of Art and A.B.K. Arnhem (Plastic Arts) 1978–85. Lives and works in Nijmegen.
Recent exhibitions include:
1989: Canon Image Centre, Amsterdam (solo). 1990: Galerie S & H de Buck, Gent; BBK Köln, Stapelhaus, Cologne. 1991: *Den Tempel*, Limburg Centre of Photography, Sittard (solo). 1992: Galerie OCCO d'Este, Amsterdam (solo). 1994: Fotogalerie Wien, Vienna.
Collections include:
Bibliothèque Nationale, Paris; Dutch Ministry of Education and Social Affairs; Dutch Photography Museum, Sittard; Provincial Library, Utrecht.

John Stezaker
pp. 28, 29

Born, Worcester, 1949. Studied at Slade School of Art, London. Lives and work in London.
Recent exhibitions include:
1983: Lisson Gallery, London (solo); *Geometry of Desire*, Das Venster, Rotterdam. 1987: Kent Fine Art, New York. 1989: *John Stezaker : The New Work*, Salama-Caro Gallery, London (solo). *John Stezaker : Neue Werke*, Friedman-Guinness Gallery, Frankfurt (solo); Glen/Dash, Los Angeles. 1990: *Film Still Collages*, F.GG, Frankfurt (solo); *Art Conceptuel, Formes Conceptuelles*, Galerie 1900/2000, Paris.
Collections include:
Arts Council of England, London; Kunstmuseum, Lucerne; Victoria and Albert Museum, London

Selected Publications:
John Stezaker : The New Work, catalogue, Salama-Caro Gallery, London, 1989; *John Stezaker*, catalogue, Friedman-Guinness Gallery, Frankfurt, 1989; *John Stezaker : Film Still Collages*, catalogue, F.GG, Frankfurt, 1990.

Thomas Struth
pp. 2–3, 86–87

Born, Geldern am Niederrhein, Germany, 1954. Studied at Kunstakademie, Düsseldorf, 1973–80. Lives and works in Düsseldorf.

Recent exhibitions include:
1990: The Renaissance Society, Chicago (solo); Marian Goodman Gallery, New York (solo); Galerie Paul Andriesse, Amsterdam (solo); *Aperto '90*, Venice Biennale; *Weitersehen 1980–1990*, Museum Haus Lange and Haus Esters, Krefeld. 1991: Galerie Meert Rihoux, Brussels (solo); Galerie Shimada, Yamaguchi (solo); *Carnegie International*, Carnegie Museum of Art, Pittsburgh. 1992: Galerie Max Hetzler, Cologne (solo); Hirshhorn Museum, Washington DC (solo); *Portraits*, Museum Haus Lange, Krefeld (solo). 1993: Hamburger Kunsthalle, Hamburg (solo); Galleria Monica de Cardenas, Milan (solo). 1994: *Thomas Struth : Photographs 1986–1992*, ICA, London (solo).

Selected publications:
Unconscious Places, Kunsthalle Bern, 1987; *Portraits*, catalogue, Marian Goodman Gallery, New York, 1990; *Portraits*, catalogue, Museum Haus Lange, Krefeld, 1992; *Museum Photographs*, Schirmer/Mosel, Munich, 1993; *Thomas Struth : Photographs*, MIT, Cambridge, Massachusetts, and Schirmer/Mosel, Munich, 1994.

Larry Sultan
pp. 42–43, 44

Born, New York, 1946. Studied at University of California (BA Political Science) 1968 and San Francisco Art Institute (MFA Photography) 1973. Lives and works in California.

Recent exhibitions include:
1991: *Pleasures and Terrors of Domestic Comfort*, Museum of Modern Art, New York and tour; *Blood Relatives*, Milwaukee Art Museum; *Imaging the Family : Photographs by Tina Barney, Lorie Novak and Larry Sultan*, List Art Center, Brown University, Rhode Island. 1992: *Dismantling The Myth of the Family*, Betty Rymer Gallery, Art Institute of Chicago; *Parents*, Museum of Contemporary Art, Wright State University, Dayton, Ohio; San Jose Museum of Art (solo). 1993: Janet Borden, Inc., New York (solo). 1994: Queen's Museum, New York (solo); Museum of Contemporary Art, San Diego (solo); Corcoran Museum of Art, Washington DC (solo).

Recent awards include:
Louis Comfort Tiffany Foundation Award, 1991. National Endowment for the Arts, Photography Fellowship, 1992. Public Art Works, Artists in Print Grant, 1992.

Collections include:
Art Institute of Chicago; Museum of Fine Arts, Houston, Texas; J. Paul Getty Museum, Los Angeles; Jewish Museum, New York; Museum of Modern Art, New York; Metropolitan Museum of Art, New York; National Museum of Art, Washington DC.

Selected publications:
Pleasures and Terrors of Domestic Comfort, catalogue, Museum of Modern Art, New York, 1991; *Blood Relatives*, catalogue, Milwaukee Art Museum, 1991; *Pictures from Home*, monograph, Harry N. Abrams, New York, 1992; *Flesh and Blood*, monograph, The Picture Project, 1992.

John R.J. Taylor
pp. 60, 61

Born, Buckie, Scotland, 1958. Studied at Duncan of Jordanstone College of Art, Dundee, and the Royal College of Art, London. Lives and works in London.

Recent exhibitions include:
1988: *Urban News City Blues*, Framework Independent Group Show, London; *The Mind*, Impressions Gallery of Photography, York and tour; Corridor Gallery, Glenrothes (solo). 1989: Duncan of Jordanstone College of Art, Dundee (solo). 1990: *Ideal Home*, Portfolio Gallery, Edinburgh (solo); *Household Choices*, Victoria and Albert Museum, London. 1992: *New Scottish Photography*, Centro Cultural del Conde Duque, Madrid.

Forthcoming commissions include:
Houston Centre for Photography, Houston, Texas: to photograph a home in Houston in the manner of the *Ideal Home* series. Commission to be exhibited alongside the *Ideal Home* exhibition in Houston, 1994.

Collections include:
Museum of Fine Arts, Texas; Museum of London; Victoria and Albert Museum, London.

Selected publications:
British Photography : Towards a Bigger Picture, Aperture Foundation Inc., New York, 1988; *Ideal Home : A detached look at modern living*, Cornerhouse Publications, Manchester, 1989; *Household Choices*, catalogue, Victoria and Albert Museum, London, and Middlesex Polytechnic, 1990; *New Scottish Photography*, catalogue, National Galleries of Scotland, 1990.

Nick Waplington
pp. 82, 83

Born, UK, 1965. Lives and works in London and Nottingham where he has worked on the *Living Room* project since 1987.

Carrie Mae Weems
pp. 84, 85

Born Portland, Oregon, 1953. Studied at California Institute of the Arts [BA] 1981; University of California, San Diego (MFA Photography) 1984; University of California, Berkeley (MA) 1984–87. Lives and works in California.

Recent exhibitions include:
1990: *Calling Out My Name*, CEPA Gallery, Buffalo, New York (solo); *Black Women Photographers*, Ten-8, London. 1991: *Biennial Exhibition*, Whitney Museum of American Art, New York; *Carrie Mae Weems*, Institute of Contemporary Art, Boston (solo); *And 22 Million Very Tired and Very Angry People*, New Museum of Contemporary Art, New York and tour (solo); *Pleasures and Terrors of Domestic Comfort*, Museum of Modern Art, New York. 1992: *Sea Islands*, PPOW, New York (solo); *Mis/Taken Identities*, University Art Museum, University of California, Santa Barbara and tour. 1993: *Carrie Mae Weems*, The National Museum of Women in the Arts, Washington DC and tour (solo). 1994: *Women's Representation of Women*, Sapporo American Center Gallery, Japan and tour; *Carrie Mae Weems*, The Hood Museum of Art, Dartmouth College, Hanover, New Hampshire (solo).

Selected publications:
Then What? Photographs and Folklore, catalogue, CEPA Gallery, Buffalo, New York, 1990; *And 22 Million Very Tired and Very Angry People*, catalogue, New Museum of Contemporary Art, New York, 1992; *Carrie Mae Weems*, catalogue, The National Museum of Women in the Arts, Washington DC, 1994.

Harry Wingfield
pp. 10, 127

Born, Denby, Derbyshire, 1910. Studied at Derby and Birmingham Schools of Art. Lives in Staffordshire.

Selected exhibitions:
Annual exhibitions, Driffold Gallery, Sutton Coldfield.

Commissions include:
Continuous commission for the design and illustration, some with text, of *Ladybird* books, 1958–81.

Selected publications:
Various children's series including Ladybird 'Keywords' Reading Scheme (*Jane and Peter*), 'Learning with Mother' and 'Talkabouts'.

Aki Yamamoto
pp. 107

Born, Kumamoto, Japan, 1966. Studied at Photographic School of London (Diploma in Photography) 1988–89 and West Surrey College of Art and Design, Farnham (BA Photography) 1990–93. Lives and works in London.

Recent exhibitions include:
1993: James Hockey Gallery, Farnham; The Mall Galleries, London. 1994: Akehurst Gallery, London, *Creative Camera* touring exhibition; Impressions Gallery, York.

Selected publications:
Creative Camera, December/January 1994. Robertson, G, (ed.), *Travellers' Tales: Narratives of Home and Displacement*, Routledge, London, 1994.

Acknowledgements

We are grateful to Michael Collins, Anna Fox, and Martin Parr, for their advice and support throughout the development of the exhibition, and acknowledge with thanks the assistance of the following:

Alexandra Artley; Nicholas Barker, BBC London; Robin Bernard, Tapestry, London; Detective Chief Inspector Biscomb, Lancashire Constabulary; Christian Boltanski; Chris Boot, Magnum Photos; David Brittain, *Creative Camera*; Ruth Charity, The Photographers' Gallery, London; Zelda Cheatle, Zelda Cheatle Gallery, London; Huw Davies, University of Sunderland; Fiona Duncan, The Photographers' Gallery Print Room, London; Ute Eskildsen, Folkwang Museum, Essen; Bruce Ferguson; Houk Friedman Gallery, New York; Beverley Friedmann, The Akehurst Gallery, London; Julian Germain, University of Sunderland; Marisela la Grave; Sunil Gupta; Peter Hall, West Surrey College of Art and Design, Farnham; Catherine af Hällström, Abo Akdemis; Martha Hanna, Canadian Museum of Contemporary Photography, Ottawa; Frank Hellsten, formerly Embassy of Finland, London; Ceri Higgins, Mexico City; Dominique Hoff, French Institute, London; Caroline Jacobs, North Parsons, London; Ian Jeffrey; Rupert Jenkins, San Francisco Camerawork; Kate Jones, Hamish Hamilton Limited, London; Susan Kismaric, The Museum of Modern Art, New York; Carry van Lakerveld; Barry Lane, Arts Council of England; Joanne Leonard, University of Michigan; Dewi Lewis, formerly of Cornerhouse, Manchester; Eva Linhoff; Jan Erik Lundström, Fotografiska Museet, Stockholm; Hildegarde Mahoney, The Photographers' Gallery, London; Laura McPhee; David Mellor, University of Sussex; Jane Morris, Phaidon Press; Anne Mossberg, Association of Female Photographers in Sweden, Stockholm; Angela Neuke, University of Essen; Gail Newton, National Gallery of Australia, Canberra; Alex Noble, South Bank Centre, London; Megan and Meri O'Mara-Williams; Sam Organ, BBC Bristol; Ian Parker, *Independent on Sunday*; Tony Parsons, North Parsons, London; Terence Pepper, National Portrait Gallery, London; Sandra Phillips, San Francisco Museum of Modern Art; Bob Portway, BBC Bristol; Christine Redmond, Gallery of Photography, Dublin; Chris Rauschenberg, Blue Sky Workshop, Portland, Oregon; Shirley Read; Michael Regan, Canada House, London; Pat Ross, Ladybird Books, Loughborough; Dirk Schweringen; Mark Sealy, Autograph, London; Margaret, Vernon and David Sproxton; Sally Stein; Paul Trevor; Catherine Turner, Special Photographers Company, London; Ritva Tähtinen, The Photographic Museum of Finland, Helsinki; Hripsime Visser, Stedelijk Museum, Amsterdam; Deborah Willis, National African American Museum Project, Washington DC; Trudy Wilner Stack, Center for Creative Photography, University of Arizona, Tucson; Paul Wombell, Impressions Gallery, York.

Barbican Art Gallery would like to thank its Corporate Members:

3i Group plc
Barings Group
The Bethlem & Maudsley NHS Trust
British Gas North Thames
British Petroleum Company plc
British Telecommunications plc
Chemical Bank
Levi's Red Tab Jeans

Nomura International
Norddeutsche Landesbank
Robert Fleming Holdings Ltd
Save & Prosper plc
Sun Alliance Group
TSB Group plc
Unilever plc
S.G. Warburg Group plc

Lenders

Barbican Art Gallery
would like to acknowledge
the assistance of:

The Arts Council of England
The Canadian High Commission, London for their
    support of Linda Duvall's installation, *Babies
    That Look Alike*
Peter Fraser, London
    for his support in printing works by The
    Boorman family and John Heatley, Lancashire
    Constabulary
The Goethe Institut, London
National Portrait Gallery, London
    for the printing of works by the Lafayette,
    London and Manchester studios
North Parsons, London
    for their support in the making of Martin
    Parr's *Love Cubes* as a floor-piece especially for
    this exhibition
Tapestry, London
    for their support in the printing of works by:
    Gerry Anderson and Doug Luke, Anthony
    Haughey, Paul Reas, Nick Waplington
Leica, Solms
    for their support of Bruce Gilden in the making
    of *Children's Birthday Parties*
The Andrew Sproxton Memorial Fund
    for its award to Paul Reas for the making of
    Portrait of an Invisible Man

The artists
Janet Borden, Inc., New York
Barbara Conway and David Brittain, London
The Stanley B. Burns M.D. Collection, New York
Coleccion 'Testimonio' – 'la Caixa', Barcelona
Scott A. Catto and Chad J. Hayduk, New York
Alan Dein, London
Kunstmuseum Düsseldorf im Ehrenhof
Susana Faja, Girona
Galerie Max Hetzler, Berlin
The Lancashire Constabulary, Preston
Tomoko and Gos Micklem
National Portrait Gallery, London
Het Nederlands Fotomuseum, Sittard
The Museum of Modern Art, New York
PPOW, New York
Telegraph Magazine, London
Hilda, June and Hilda Thompson, Preston
Val Williams, London

But Kay and Gerda went on, hand in hand: and as they
went, beautiful spring was all about them with blossom and
greenery. The church bells rang out, and they saw the tall
towers and the big town – the very one where they lived —
and into it they came and away to their grandmother's door,
and up the stairs and into the room, where everything stood
where it did before, and the clock was saying 'Tick, tick', and
the hands turning round. But, just as they passed through the
door they were aware that they were grown people. The roses
in the gutter were flowering in at the open windows, and there
were the little stools, and Kay and Gerda sat down each on
their own, and held each other by the hand. They had
forgotten the cold empty splendour of the Snow Queen's
palace as if it were a dismal dream.

from *The Snow Queen*
in *Hans Christian Andersen : Forty-Two Stories*
Translated by M.R.James
Faber and Faber Ltd. London, 1968

Harry Wingfield
illustration
from *Light, Mirrors
and Lenses*
Ladybird Junior Science Book
1962

Published by Barbican Art Gallery
to accompany the exhibition
Who's Looking at the Family?

26 May – 4 September 1994

Barbican Art Gallery
Barbican Centre
London EC2Y 8DS

Organised by
Carol Brown, Brigitte Lardinois
and Donna Loveday,
Barbican Art Gallery

Barbican Art Gallery
is owned, funded and managed
by the Corporation of London

  GOETHE-INSTITUT

Designed by Richard Hollis

Typeset in Monotype Plantin
Printed in an edition of 1,500 copies
by BAS Printers Limited,
Over Wallop, Hampshire

Photographs by
Downtown Darkroom, p. 57
Brian Russell, pp. 10, 20-21, 48, 127
Grant Kernan AK Photos, pp. 32-33
Jonathan Morris Ebbs, pp. 25, 108-9

© Corporation of London
Text:
Val Williams and authors quoted
Faber and Faber Limited

The extract from W.H. Auden's poem pp. 2–3
is from *The English Auden*, Mendelson, E, (ed.),
Faber and Faber Limited, London 1977

Images:
The artists
National Portrait Gallery, London
The Chief Constable, Lancashire Constabulary
The Thompson family

ISBN 0-946372-32-2

9 780946 372324